KITCHEN MEMORIES

KITCHEN MEMORIES

FOOD AND KITCHEN LIFE 1837–1939

COMPILED BY ELIZABETH DRURY AND PHILIPPA LEWIS
FROM THE AMORET TANNER EPHEMERA COLLECTION

 THE NATIONAL TRUST

Mixed Sources
Product group from well-managed
forests and other controlled sources
www.fsc.org   Cert no. SGS-COC-004105
© 1996 Forest Stewardship Council

FSC

First published in the United Kingdom in 2009 by
National Trust Books
10 Southcombe Street
London W14 0RA

An imprint of Anova Books Company Ltd

ISBN 9781905400829

A CIP catalogue for this book is available from the British Library.

15 14 13 12 10 09
10 9 8 7 6 5 4 3 2 1

Repro by Rival Colour Ltd, UK
Printed by SNP Leefung Printers Ltd, China

This book can be ordered direct from the publisher at the website www.anovabooks.com,
or try your local bookshop. Also available at National Trust shops.

CONTENTS

INTRODUCTION

Kitchen Memories is an evocation of the English kitchen during the century between the accession of Queen Victoria and the eve of the Second World War. It is illustrated with ephemera, the small, incidental bits of printed flotsam and jetsam that are normally thrown away, but for some reason have survived. Maybe they were tucked into a cookery book to mark a page, jammed at the back of a drawer or perhaps saved for their colour or funny shape. Labels, bill-heads, give-away advertisements, recipe leaflets, menu cards, cuttings from magazines, milk-bottle tops, old packets, and the odd envelope and paper bag – all transport us straight back into a kitchen of 1837 or 1937 in a way that grander historical documents do not. They have the immediacy of a snapshot taken on an impulse. They are the very texture of everyday life of long ago.

To a cook trying to look into the future from her Victorian kitchen, the changes, as with any span of one hundred years or so, would be unimaginable. Even in a middling sort of household the kitchen area would have been a place bursting with life, from crack of dawn to late evening; from the first duty of lighting the big black coal range to the last of wearily scouring the heavy iron pans in tepid water drawn from a pump and heated in a kettle. How could such a cook have foreseen the sootless kitchen with smooth, brightly coloured surfaces, heat and light at the flick of a switch, and the

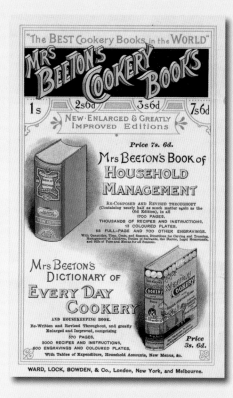

Above: Mrs Beeton's name endured in numerous versions and editions of the original 1861 Beeton's Book of Household Management. *Some were advertised in c.1905 at prices ranging from 1s to 7s 6d.*

empty labour-saved hours before she popped in to prepare the next meal? So much less food, so much less work and with this, perhaps, many lost skills. Coal power and elbow grease are replaced by electricity and convenience.

To keep a Victorian kitchen running, to scrub and clean, to chop and boil, to fetch and carry, there were servants. They were the responsibility of the mistress of a Victorian household, to be employed within the constraints of her husband's income and therefore her budget. She set down their duties and supervised them at their work. This could be a situation of tension and fearfulness, as cartoons in *Punch* and much literature testify. However, to employ a maid-of-all-work or general servant, for whom cooking was just one of her many tasks, was an ambition – indeed a necessity – for those of quite modest means: on £150 a year in the 1860s this should have been possible. Middle-class families living in the larger terraced houses and urban villas would keep at the least a cook with some degree of experience, a kitchen maid and a housemaid. In grander establishments the staff would include a housekeeper, a butler, a cook and a bevy of helpers in the kitchen, the most junior being the scullery-maid, who might be as young as eight years of age.

As time went by, it became increasingly unlikely that the type of person who employed a general servant could afford more than a 'daily'. The mistress of the house might have a charwoman to do the cleaning and odd jobs, but it is probable that she would have

Above: Selection of breakfast and tea china suitable for the average household, including a sandwich box and bacon dish, from a late Victorian edition of Mrs Beeton.

taken on the cooking, as well as the washing and ironing, herself. In 1913 Mrs Frazer, the author of *First Aid to the Servantless*, wrote that the 'owners of ample means must have servants just as they must have motor cars, hunters and pictures, caviare and pineapples.' Otherwise, in her opinion, only the untidy, who are always late and in a muddle, and the lazy needed servants, and the 'cross-grained': 'Ill-tempered people who are addicted to domestic squabbles, are restrained in their outbursts by the maid, who stands in front of the sideboard and who watches her employers as a cat watches mice.'

The change, as it were, from kitchen maid to electric toaster, is reflected in the scale of food preparation in the kitchen. The Victorian cook might follow the instructions given in a small volume of 1886 called *Breakfast Dishes for Every Morning of Three Months*, which suggested that for Saturday, February 18th Fried Salsify in Batter, Reindeers' Tongues and Cowheel Fried should be offered, as well as Poached Egg and Bacon, Breakfast Cakes with Anchovy and Strawberry Jam. This is a far cry from Corn Flakes, the '30-second breakfast', advertised in 1939 and accompanied by the quote from Mrs Hall of Preston, Lancs, 'I like Kellogg's too – they need no cooking so I save time and there is no messy saucepan to wash up.'

In the 19th century, the cook was constrained by what was in season. The railway sped watercress from Hampshire and turkeys from Norfolk to London, but generally she had to keep constant vigilance on the freshness of her food. Refrigeration brought about

Above: Making the Victorian maid's life easier, the Guinea Furbator knife cleaner exhibited in London in 1862 by Hilliard & Chapman.

a revolution, not only on a domestic scale but also nationally, as frozen meat and dairy produce shipped from the other side of the world helped with shortages and lowered prices, as well as introducing new and out-of-season produce. Victorian store cupboards and larders contained home-pickled and salted meat, fish and vegetables, and carefully stored eggs and cheese. But as the 19th century turned into the 20th, shelves were more likely to be stacked with tins and packets of ready-made and easy-to-use foods. Some brands, such as Bisto gravy, Heinz baked beans and Bird's custard, became embedded in the nation's diet. This range of goods was delivered by a change in retailing. Small specialist tradesmen were being replaced by chains of grocery stores on high streets that could 'pile it high and sell it cheap'. Companies such as Home & Colonial Stores, Maypole and Lipton's had trading partners around the world.

There were always strong voices giving out advice and guidance. The most famous in Victorian times was Isabella Beeton, whose readers were mainly middle-class housewives, whose aim was to improve the family's position in society – or at least to keep up appearances. *Beeton's Book of Household Management*, first published in 1861, sold more than 60,000 copies in its first year. Recipes were gleaned from earlier publications, such as those of Eliza Acton and Alexis Soyer, and from the *Englishwoman's Domestic Magazine* published by Mrs Beeton's husband; these were recipes sent in from the kitchens of the magazine's readers and reprinted in the book after they had been tried, tested and adapted in her own kitchen.

Above: Soap advertisement of c.1885 points up the divisions between 'upstairs' and 'downstairs', suggesting that efficient soap promoted harmonious relations between the two.

Among the recipes were some for the plainest food suitable for children and invalids – Boiled Bread Pudding and Eel Soup – and some for the grandest, fanciest food – Pig's Feet with Truffles and Pheasants à la Financière. There were bills of fare for family dinners, larger dinners for up to 18 persons throughout the year and a cold collation for a ball supper for 70 or 80 (also for serving at a summer entertainment or a wedding or christening breakfast). Numerous versions, adaptations and updates of the original work were published after her death in 1865. Generations of housewives and cooks have been reassured to feel that they could turn for advice to a copy of Mrs Beeton.

From the middle of the 19th century, the better-off readers of Mrs Beeton were enjoying a period of unparalleled plenty. Goods were being manufactured and sold on an almost unimaginable scale, and there was choice in everything, from a toasting fork to a garden spade. Consumption was huge, and this included the consumption of food. Dinner consisted of numerous courses and prepared dishes. At the same time as taking account of this abundance, Mrs Beeton placed much emphasis on frugality and economy, and included in *Household Management* is the total price of the ingredients for each recipe and the length of time it would take to cook, together with an indication of the cost in fuel. One of her cakes had the title 'Economical'.

Almost all Victorian cookery books have a section on using up food and leftovers, on rechauffées, patties, rissoles and hashes. It is probable that some of the remainders ended up in the households

Above: Elaborate Victorian dishes were time consuming to prepare: Cassell's Dictionary of Cookery displays at the top a Garnished Chartreuse of Partridges.

of the poor. Scraps were given away to the needy, who called at the back door. In an increasingly urban Britain, large swathes of the population lived in extreme poverty, in overcrowded slums with no means of cooking except on an open fire. Scenes to arouse the consciences of the well-to-do were sketched out by writers such as Charles Dickens and Henry Mayhew in his book *London Labour and the London Poor*, published in 1851.

Thought was given on how to nourish the poor by two of the leading chefs of the Victorian era. Alexis Soyer published *Soyer's Charitable Cookery, or The Poor Man's Regenerator* in 1848, and Charles Elmé Francatelli's *A Plain Cookery Book for the Working Classes* came out in 1852. Francatelli, who succeeded Soyer as chef at the Reform Club in London (having had a brief and not altogether satisfactory spell as chief cook to Queen Victoria), published *The Cook's Guide and Housekeeper's and Butler's Assistant* in the same year as *Mrs Beeton's Book of Household Management* made its appearance.

Soyer was an influential figure. He promoted the use of gas for cooking and created his own range of patent culinary utensils (Baking Stewing Pan, Improved Baking Dish, Vegetable Drainer and Portfolio Meat Screen), which were promoted by Mary Jewry in *Warne's Model Cookery and Housekeeping Book* of 1869. The same route to commercial success was taken by Agnes Marshall, who ran a cookery school in London's Mortimer Street attended by both mistresses and their cooks. Her adjacent showroom displayed and sold the very latest in cooking equipment – some of it patented by

Above: Manufacturers frequently promoted their products with elegantly printed and die-cut scraps, bookmarks, calendars and collectible postcards.

her – and products such as her own brand of gelatine. She maximised her position – and profits – with cookery books such as *Mrs A. B. Marshall's Cookery Book*, published in 1888, and her *Book of Ices* of *c.*1898; she also ran an agency for cooks.

In contrast to the definitive, and rather expensive, tomes that were available, there were any number of small recipe books and leaflets put out by companies, manufacturers and organisations, and no women's magazine lacked recipe pages. Most were destined for the dust-cart or the fire, but some were carefully clipped and saved. So we have the survival of the 2d booklet *Fish Cookery* published by British Dominions Insurance Co. (*c.*1911), the *Atora Book of Olde Time Christmas Customs, Games and Recipes* (*c.*1925) and the Newark Inter-Denominational Union for Social Service publication *Hints and Recipes for Cooking To-Day* (1915). This last gave much-needed advice on cooking during the shortages of the First World War: 'In order that workers may keep their strength to efficiently do their labour, they must have a good substitute for Meat,' it commented, recommending split peas, butter and haricot beans, red lentils and cheese.

New names emerged giving guidance on ways to run a kitchen, and to enjoy the new technologies of cooking with gas and electricity. Agnes Jekyll wrote a column in

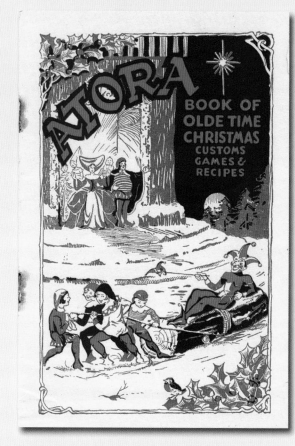

Above: With the compliments of the manufacturers of Atora. The booklet included recipes for Christmas Pudding, Mincemeat and Turkey Stuffing, all using their beef suet.

The Times, pieces that were published in 1922 as *Kitchen Essays with Recipes and their Occasions*; she clearly answered a need felt by the loss of the old order of cooks and maids that disappeared rapidly after the First World War. As Jekyll put it, 'when homes dissolve and re-form, or the main prop of the household is withdrawn, it is often found that a good tradition or a valued formula, painstakingly acquired, has vanished beyond recovery ... We have grown accustomed to shorter meals, and to prefer them – to do without things which we now realise were never necessities.' Her motto was 'Little and Good', and she urged the use of oven-to-table wares and discouraged over-elaboration of food: 'games of dominoes played in truffles over the chicken cream, birds' nests counterfeited round the poached eggs and castellated cakes', she regarded as a misdirection of energy.

As typical of her time as Isabella Beeton was of hers, was the writer and journalist Elizabeth Craig, who wrote from her own direct experience of being a passionate cook. Her first cookery feature was for the *Daily Express* in 1920; the first of her many books came out three years later. She was in demand as an endorser of food products and kitchen equipment, and in 1930 wrote *250 Recipes with Borwick's Baking Powder* and in 1934 *The Importance of Eating Potatoes* for the Potato Marketing Board. Throughout her prodigious output she never failed to understand that she was addressing the housewife as cook and provider. While she might urge them to be skilled jam and chutney makers, and to become a 'Queen of the Preserving Pan', she also appreciated that, 'When a meal is wanted in 5 minutes, fly to the nearest delicatessen shop and titivate what you buy at home before serving it.'

Above: Advertisement for Jaffa Oranges, c.1930, promoting them as a source of vitamins 'to guard your health'.

THE VICTORIAN COOK

'Cook Wanted – a respectable middle-aged person, of strict integrity and cleanly industrious habits, who well understands making bread, pastry, soups, &c. her business generally, and management with care and economy.' *The Times*, 1847

Domestic staff were acquired by advertising, by word of mouth and through the help of an agency. One such agency was Miss Harrison's. Using her services, a householder could be reasonably sure that the certificate supplied by a former employer attesting to an applicant's honest, sober and moral character was genuine. (A gentleman's character reference of a female servant was always to be distrusted.)

Cooks were ranked according to their experience and expertise. At the lowest end of the scale was the maid-of-all-work, or general servant, who was employed by spinsters, widowed persons and families of modest means. A cook-general shared the cleaning with a housemaid as well as cooking; a 'plain' cook was capable of cooking unadventurous everyday fare, and had a kitchen maid and perhaps a scullery-maid working under her. A 'professed' cook was responsible for dishes that were complicated in their preparation and elaborate in their appearance, with some special dishes in her armoury. A male chef (usually French) was employed only in the grandest establishments.

Left: Booklet of 1892 setting out terms of work for female servants registered with Miss Harrison's offices in Manchester.

Below: Victorian cook and housemaid posing for a photograph in their employer's garden.

COOK AND MISTRESS

The mistress of the house was in some measure at the mercy of her cook. Nothing was more shameful and more likely to incur the wrath of the master of the house than unpunctual meals and bad food: 'ill-cooked food, monotonous food, insufficient food, injure the physique, and ruin the temper.' A subject of Victorian satire was the young housewife terrorised by her bad-tempered cook.

But there was always the other kind. Characterised as cosy and rosy cheeked, her apron starched and spotlessly white, she generated a sense of well-being throughout the home. Good, well-presented food was sent in to the dining room, reliably on time. She discussed the day's menu amicably with her mistress, and in some instances worked alongside her in the kitchen. She welcomed visitors, turning a blind eye to the kitchen-maids' followers – expressly forbidden in most households – and was not averse to a doorstep encounter herself.

The cook's day was long, starting early and as soon as the fire was lit. After an hour or two of peace and quiet in the afternoon, activity in the kitchen reached its peak in the early evening. When visitors were expected, the dinner had to reflect well on her employers, and enhance their standing and reputation.

Above: Cook and mistress in an advertisement of c.1890 for Albene, a superior cooking fat obtainable from a grocer or a chemist.

CONTENTMENT   HAPPINESS

FLETCHER RUSSELL & CO

WARRINGTON
MANCHESTER & LONDON
COPYRIGHT

Above: Cook at the top of steps to the basement passing the time of day with a policeman on the beat, a postcard from the set Familiar Figures of London, *c.1910.*

Above: Cook's contentment with cooking on a gas stove and the diners' happiness at the resulting dish. A leaflet of c.1900–1905 from the manufacturers of gas appliances Fletcher Russell & Co.

Left: Liebig advertisement printed in The Illustrated London News *in the 1890s. The meat extract was used to flavour sauces and soups.*

COOK AND HOUSEWIFE

The 20th-century cook benefited from a huge reduction in the physical labour involved in cooking. This was brought about by the arrival in the home of gas and electricity, which powered new machines and new gadgets. Whether she was a housewife providing for her own family or a cook working unassisted in her employer's kitchen, she was finding that she could prepare and cook food with greater speed and reliability. It was now possible to 'run up' something to eat.

Women's magazines started up giving useful hints on how to manage a household: *Woman's Weekly* in 1911 – 'practical and useful' was its motto; *Good Housekeeping* in 1922; *Woman's Own* in 1932; and *Woman* in 1937. Cookery books containing simple recipes were produced in association with, for instance, MacDougall's the flour manufacturers, the electricity and gas companies, and the new schools of domestic science; packaged and tinned foods also helped with instant solutions to a meal. Everywhere, the idea of convenience was being promoted.

In 1936 Mrs Craig assured the cook-hostess, 'It is nonsense to imagine that you have to serve half a dozen courses to please your guests. Then, make the shops help you all they can. See that any fowls come home cleaned and trussed as you want them, larded as required.'

Above: Modern Ten-Minute Recipes *compiled for Radiation Ltd, manufacturers of New World Gas Cookers, by Mrs C. S. Peel. The booklet was handed out to customers in the early 1920s.*

Thermostove

PATENT. REG.DESIGN.

What you can do with ONE FIRE.

Manufactured only by the Pioneers in the design of
OPEN-FIRE DOMESTIC BOILERS
HARTLEY & SUGDEN LTD
Atlas Works, HALIFAX, England.
LIST T.8.

*Above: The Thermostove booklet of c.1925
extolled the advantages to the cook of a
single, compact apparatus in the kitchen
serving as boiler as well as cooker.*

*Above: The 'sympathetically
designed cabinet' of 1921 from the
Quicksey Cabinet Manufacturing
Co. made all the requirements for
preparing food within easy reach.*

*Left: Cook putting a joint into the
oven of the Valor-Perfection Oil
Cooking Stove, which was easy
to light, clean and move. An
advertisement from the magazine
The Ideal Home, 1922.*

THE KITCHEN

So that no smell of cooking or sound of clattering pans and chattering servants was heard, the Victorian kitchen was usually tucked away in the basement or at the back of the house. What lay behind the proverbial 'green baize door' was a place apart. Connected to the kitchen might be a series of rooms – a scullery for cleaning vegetables and all the dirty jobs, a store room, a larder and a pantry.

Where there was no servants' hall, the domestic staff sat and ate their meals in the kitchen. There would be a chair or two, usually of the Windsor type. The cook might be given a bedroom in the attic but the other servants would often lie down to sleep on a mat in front of the range.

The centrepiece of every kitchen was the kitchen table, a sturdy piece of furniture with a scrubbed deal top; elbow grease, soda, soft soap and fuller's earth produced the desired whiteness. Here the ingredients were assembled and prepared, by chopping and slicing, pounding and rolling, sifting and mixing. And here too the cooked food, dished up and ready to be taken to the dining table, was set out in the order in which it was to be presented.

Left: The Kitchen, a Liebig advertising insert of c.1890 with the 'perfect' cook in her 'perfect' place of work.

Above: Cook and housemaid resting beside the kitchen fire, in front of which a joint is roasting, suspended from a line attached to a wind-up bottle jack. Punch *cartoon of 1853.*

Right: Advertising insert for Liebig's Extract of Beef from the 1890s showing a range with cooking pots, dresser and kitchen table typically to be found in a Victorian kitchen.

Below: Kitchen furniture, illustrated with prices, in the Crowden & Garrod catalogue of 1903. The Strong Arm Chair would be drawn up to the table at mealtimes from its place beside the fire or range.

Strong Arm Chair, **9/6**   **4/3** each, six for **24/-**   Kitchen Tables, a large variety of sizes and shapes, from **12/6**

THE KITCHEN RANGE

The cook's nerves and the well-being of the entire household depended on the performance of the kitchen range. These cast-iron monsters required a great deal of coaxing and chivvying to produce of their best. Lugging the coal, raking out the ashes and cinders, blackleading and polishing were wearisome tasks.

Open ranges had a basket for an exposed fire, over which were hung cooking pots and joints of meat. With closed ranges, or 'kitcheners', which were in use from the mid-19th century until well into the following century, the heat was channelled in order to give an even heat to the ovens and boiler. Ranges with self-filling boilers were the best: 'The brain of no modern cook is equal to remembering to refill in good time a boiler that does not fill itself,' wrote Mrs Haweis, the author of *The Art of Housekeeping*, in 1889, 'and when the boiler wants to burst, it selects the most inconvenient times.'

Later models, such as the prize-winning Eagle Composite, had much to recommend them, but the compact Thermostove, which burned coke or anthracite rather than coal, undertook all forms of cooking, ensured a continuous and abundant supply of hot water, and was more efficient still.

Above: Advertisement of c.1880 for Caswell & Bowden's coal. Filling and carrying heavy coal scuttles was one of the most tiring and tedious of household tasks.

Below: Illustration from the 1885 catalogue of the prize-winning Eagle ranges, showing hot air from the fire travelling through flues to heat the roasting and pastry ovens.

Left: The Utilis Kitchener, c.1895. 'Open or closed fire, Capacious ovens adapted either for roasting or baking.'

THE GOLD MEDAL EAGLE RANGE.
OVEN FLUES.

Perfect Bottom Heat for Pastry Baking.

Roasting Oven perfectly ventilated with Hot Air.

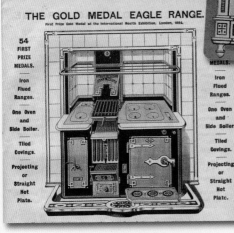

THE GOLD MEDAL EAGLE RANGE.
First Prize Gold Medal at the International Health Exhibition, London, 1884.

54 FIRST PRIZE MEDALS.

Iron Flued Ranges.

One Oven and Side Boiler.

Tiled Covings.

Projecting or Straight Hot Plate.

MEDALS.

Iron Flued Ranges.

One Oven and Side Boiler.

Tiled Covings.

Projecting or Straight Hot Plate.

Left: Advertising insert from the late 19th century for Oakey's bottled black for 'preserving and beautifying' the surface of all types of stove and grate.

OAKEY'S
WELLINGTON

For preserving and beautifying Stoves, Grates, Chimney Corners, Fenders, and all kinds of Ironwork, &c., &c.

In Bottles
6d., 1s. and 2s. each.
AND IN HALF GALLON AND ONE GALLON CANS

BRUNSWICK BLACK

OAKEY'S
WELLINGTON

Superior Quality, producing a Black Enamel Surface on Stoves, Grates, Fenders and Ironwork, Wood, Leather, and all Metals.

Sold in Bottles at
6d., 1s. and 2s.
Each.
And in Half Gallon and One Gallon Cans

BERLIN BLACK

Above: Range manufactured by The Eagle Range & Gas Stove Co. Ltd, Bristol. On the left is the boiler with a tap for the supply of hot water and at the top a rack for warming plates.

POTS AND PANS

Roasting, frying, glazing, boiling and broiling, stewing, sautéing and steaming – the full gamut of cooking processes required a substantial array of pots and pans to produce the quantity of dishes required for a dinner of four or five courses. Cooking times were lengthy (pea soup, four hours). *Warne's Model Cookery and Housekeeping book* of 1869 listed 37 saucepans and kettles 'absolutely required by a good Cook'. They included six enamel stewpans; a stock pot; pans for sautéing and braising, for making omelette soufflés and for preserving; oval, round and 'bachelor's' frying pans; fish kettles for turbot, mackerel and salmon; a *bain-marie* for keeping sauces hot; and three different kinds of 'digesters'. Digesters, patented by Mr Slack, were pressure cookers. Captain Warren's Everybody's Cooking Pot was similarly economical with fuel, the claim being that a 10lb leg of mutton could be cooked in three hours and remain succulent, however indifferent the cook.

Above and left: Captain Warren's Everybody's Cooking Pot, a steamer, advertised as simultaneously making every fibre of meat tender and producing nourishing soup.

Heavy cast-iron pots, soon soot-blackened, were standard for use on ranges, but needed to be watched for rust and holes; very expensive copper pans could cause poisoning if the tin lining eroded and the copper was exposed to vinegar or acid. From the 1840s enamelled pans were available, but these tended to chip and were apt to leach lead. The 1903 edition of Mrs Beeton favoured wrought steel as it was easy to keep clean and did not discolour food.

BAIN MARIE PAN

Above: Copper bain-marie pan, 'valuable in families where regularity and punctuality in meals cannot be depended upon.' Illustration from Warne's Model Cookery and Housekeeping Book, *1869.*

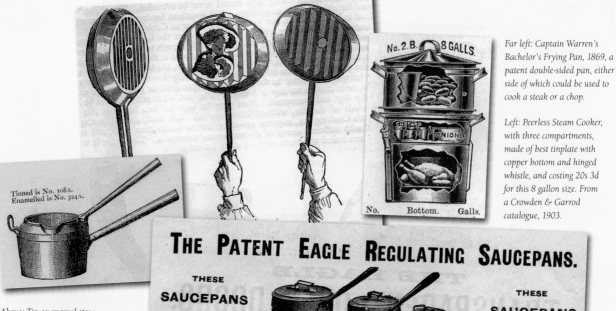

Far left: Captain Warren's Bachelor's Frying Pan, 1869, a patent double-sided pan, either side of which could be used to cook a steak or a chop.

Left: Peerless Steam Cooker, with three compartments, made of best tinplate with copper bottom and hinged whistle, and costing 20s 3d for this 8 gallon size. From a Crowden & Garrod catalogue, 1903.

Tinned is No. 108A.
Enamelled is No. 324A.

Above: Tin or enamel stew, porridge or milk pot, manufactured by J. & J. Siddons of West Bromwich, 'guaranteed free from lead, arsenic, zinc'. Leaflet of c.1880.

THE PATENT EAGLE REGULATING SAUCEPANS.

THESE SAUCEPANS WILL BOIL EITHER FAST OR SLOW AS REQUIRED.

THESE SAUCEPANS WILL BOIL EITHER FAST OR SLOW AS REQUIRED.

Above: Late 19th-century Patent Eagle Regulating Saucepans for kitchen ranges. The stands lifted the pans from contact with the stove, thereby reducing the heat.

Salmon or Jack Kettle.   Turbot Kettle.   Fish Kettle.

Left: Fish kettles illustrated in Warne's Model Cookery and Housekeeping Book, which describes turbot as the finest and most expensive flat fish, generally weighing 5–20lb.

THE VICTORIAN KITCHEN

The 'great laboratory of every household' was how the kitchen was described in early editions of Mrs Beeton. Taking pride of place was the kitchen dresser fitted with ledges displaying plates and dishes, and hooks for cups and jugs of various sizes; in larger establishments the 'upstairs' china was kept separate, with the plate and the glass in the pantry. Deep drawers for dishcloths, cloths for steamed puddings and a tablecloth for kitchen meals were to be found below, and some dressers had cupboards for bowls and the like.

Glazed tiles that were easy to keep clean were recommended for the walls, upon which were hung various kitchen implements and utensils. The stone flags on the floor of a typical basement kitchen were hard on the feet and punishingly cold; strategically placed wooden duckboards went some way to reducing the discomfort.

Mrs Beeton insisted on punctuality, and Anne Cobbett, who wrote *The English Housekeeper* in 1842 'for the person of moderate income', thought that every prudent housekeeper should keep the kitchen clock under lock and key to frustrate 'that good understanding which sometimes subsists between the clock and the cook, and which is brought about by the instrumentality of a broom-handle, or some such magic'.

Above: Calendar for 1897 with the picture of a kitchen dresser, or a cupboard with the doors closed, an advertisement for Sunlight Soap, manufactured by Lever Brothers from 1885.

Left: Leaflet of 1910 advertising Panshine, for cleaning everything except clothes. Inside are instructions on how to clean marble and tiles, cutlery, and pots and pans.

KITCHEN MAGIC

1D.

PANSHINE

FOR EVERYTHING BUT CLOTHES

Patentees —
H. D. Pochin & Co. Ltd
MANCHESTER.

LAMP SHADES, COOKING STOVES.
TILES, DINNER TABLE & MARBLE.

THIS IS THE LABEL REFUSE ALL OTHERS

DO YOU WANT TO SEE KITCHEN MAGIC?

THEN LOOK INSIDE

RIGG DESIGN

The Happiness of the *Drawing Room* depends upon the Comfort in the *Kitchen.*

Right: Plates, kept either on the dresser or in a cupboard in the country, from an illustration in a late 19th-century edition of Mrs Beeton.

Above: Advertising postcard of 1903 for Hudson's Soap, used for washing up and for washing clothes. It depicts a typical turn-of-the-century kitchen.

GAS COOKERS

When in 1841 Alexis Soyer, one of the famous chefs of the Victorian age, installed gas ovens in the kitchens of the Reform Club in London they were a source of wonder, and he was quick to praise their economy: 'they are not lit till the moment wanted ... and may be put out the moment it is done with'. Small gas cookers suitable for domestic kitchens were on show at the Great Exhibition of 1851, but it was only after gas companies introduced penny-in-the-slot gas meters and rental schemes for cookers several decades later that householders became convinced of their advantages: namely the supply piped automatically into the house and the ease with which the cooking temperatures could be regulated to boil or simmer.

William Sugg was one of the most successful manufacturers of gas stoves: 'Sugg's gas stoves can do everything except talk,' stated the *Daily Telegraph* in 1888; Marie Jenny Sugg was the author in 1890 of the first gas cookery book, *The Art of Cooking by Gas*. She assured readers they would 'find themselves freed of trouble, dirt and uncertainty'. Companies competed to offer such improvements as grills, plate racks, removable shelves and a choice of coloured enamel finishes, and a universal standard 'regulo' of heat was introduced.

Above and left: Gas cookers were sold or rented through the showrooms of local gas companies. Brentford Gas Company promoted Parkinson Cookers with this novelty advertisement of c.1900.

SUGG'S "CHARING CROSS" GAS KITCHENER.

PATENT

FRYING

WILLIAM SUGG'S PATENT

CHOPS STEAKS

FISH &c

"FLASH LIGHT" SERVICE

ENAMELLED

HOT AIR OVEN

ENAMELLED

TOILET PAGE SERVICE

ENAMELLED

"THE BEST TO BE OBTAINED."—Vide "The Pictorial World,"
June 3, 1886.

May be seen in action and tested at the SHOW ROOMS—
WILLIAM SUGG & CO., Limited, Charing Cross.

RECIPES

COOKERY BOOK

PLAN YOUR
perfect kitchen
round this perfect
Cooker . . . . Automatic Oven-Heat Control . . . Glass-
like enamel inside and outside, back and front . . . Glass-
finishes—Green and Cream, Blue and White Deluxe, Mottle and
Grey Dapple . . . Specially designed plate rack . . . Patent hotplate
which prevents pans rocking and spilling . . . Stainless taps.
    The ideal cooker upon which to build the heart of the home—the
kitchen. Think what hygiene the gleaming enamel means. It will not
harbour dust and grease—a wipe with a damp cloth is all that is required to keep it spotless. And what successful dishes can be cooked
when you can control the oven heat better than the greatest cook
alive—simply by setting the "MAINSTAT." Undoubtedly the MAIN
is the last word in cookers.

THE MAINSTAT

From the moment of ignition
the gas, the "MAINSTAT"
affects full flow until its right
oven-heat is reached. It then
keeps the oven at the correct
heat until the food is cooked.

FREE BOOKLET COUPON
Please send me a free copy of your Recipe
Booklet.
Name ....
Address ....
R. & A. MAIN LIMITED (Dept. 22)
48 Grosvenor Gardens, London, S.W.1

ENAMELLED *Gas Cookers*

*Above: Advertisement for William
Sugg's Gas Kitchener, late 1880s.
Joints were roasted by hanging
them in the oven from a hook.*

*Right: Gas burners dating from the
1860s. They were used in conjunction
with the kitchen range and could
reliably boil a kettle fast.*

*Above: Gas cooker
manufactured by R. W.
Main Ltd, in a choice of
green and cream or blue
and white enamel,
advertised in Modern
Home magazine in 1936.*

KITCHEN UTENSILS

For cooking on an open range, a trivet, a gridiron, griddles, a toasting fork, tongs and a dripping pan were required. A bottle-jack, to be hung from a movable bar attached to the mantelpiece, and a screen, were used for roasting; from a bottle-jack described as large enough for regular family use could be suspended 20lb of meat.

Spoons and ladles, dishing-up forks, meat saws, cleavers and skewers, knives in various sizes, and implements for scooping and peeling, scraping and straining were among the articles advertised as essential to the cook. Sugar was bought in loaf form in Victorian times and needed to be cut with sugar nippers; breadcrumbs were made with a rasp and spices ground using a pestle and mortar; roasts were kept warm under dish covers; a wire or horsehair sieve was required to make smooth purées and soups. 'More money is usually wasted in cooking by guessing than by careless shopping and storing,' wrote Mrs Craig. For 'Foolproof Cookery', measuring spoons, a standard measuring cup, and a quart and a gill measure were indispensable. And no kitchen was properly equipped without a set of scales and weights.

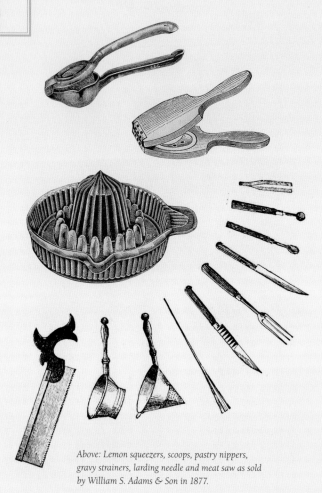

Above: Lemon squeezers, scoops, pastry nippers, gravy strainers, larding needle and meat saw as sold by William S. Adams & Son in 1877.

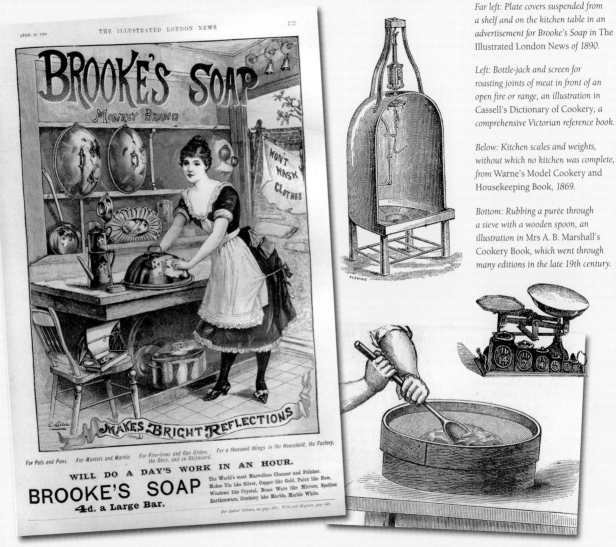

Far left: Plate covers suspended from a shelf and on the kitchen table in an advertisement for Brooke's Soap in The Illustrated London News of 1890.

Left: Bottle-jack and screen for roasting joints of meat in front of an open fire or range, an illustration in Cassell's Dictionary of Cookery, a comprehensive Victorian reference book.

Below: Kitchen scales and weights, without which no kitchen was complete, from Warne's Model Cookery and Housekeeping Book, 1869.

Bottom: Rubbing a purée through a sieve with a wooden spoon, an illustration in Mrs A. B. Marshall's Cookery Book, which went through many editions in the late 19th century.

KITCHEN GADGETS

Chopping, mincing, peeling, shelling, whipping, slicing, squeezing, stoning, coring and beating were all tedious and time-consuming tasks to be done by hand in Victorian times, frequently by a sorely put-upon and hard-pressed kitchen maid. Inventors and manufacturers rose to the occasion, however, and in the spirit of the age produced an array of useful gadgets intended to make light work of these processes.

One of the most ingenious pieces of engineering on a small scale was a slicer for French beans manufactured by Spong & Co.; another was a machine for chopping meat, sold by the London firm of Lyon, which incorporated hot-water bottles to keep the food hot while it was being cut up, 'to assist digestion'. Coffee grinders, apple and potato peelers, a device for stoning raisins and one for shelling peas were other inventions. The rotary whisk was a step up on the old wire whisk.

There was a general reluctance, though, to use these new-fangled devices. In a little late 19th-century book entitled *Home Comforts*, the author criticised those responsible for managing the household and their servants for clinging to the old practices 'because it was my mother's way'. Not to use the very latest kitchen gadgets was a false economy.

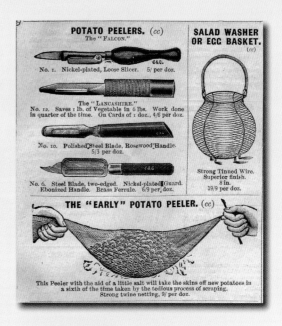

Above: Gadgets from Crowden & Garrod's 1903 catalogue, including an ingenious potato peeler made of twine netting.

Above: Tin openers, including one in the form of a bull's head (shown top).

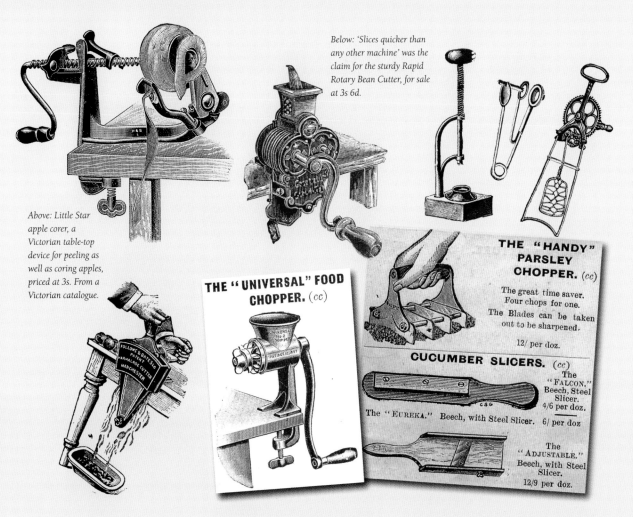

Below: 'Slices quicker than any other machine' was the claim for the sturdy Rapid Rotary Bean Cutter, for sale at 3s 6d.

Above: Little Star apple corer, a Victorian table-top device for peeling as well as coring apples, priced at 3s. From a Victorian catalogue.

THE "UNIVERSAL" FOOD CHOPPER. (cc)

THE "HANDY" PARSLEY CHOPPER. (cc)

The great time saver. Four chops for one. The Blades can be taken out to be sharpened.

12/ per doz.

CUCUMBER SLICERS. (cc)

The "FALCON." Beech, Steel Slicer. 4/6 per doz.

The "EUREKA." Beech, with Steel Slicer. 6/ per doz

The "ADJUSTABLE." Beech, with Steel Slicer. 12/9 per doz.

Above: Patent Marmalade Machine that could cut three oranges a minute and was described as supplying a 'long-felt want'.

Above: Universal Food Chopper. Fitted with three cutters and with all the parts tinned, it 'Chops Meat or Suet coarse or fine.' The price was 5s 6d.

Above: Plum Stoners and the Express Dover Egg Beater, 'with the action of a fork' (top); Parsley Chopper and Cucumber Slicers. From Crowden & Garrod's catalogue, 1903.

CLEANING AND POLISHING

In large establishments, the cleaning and polishing of the household plate, and all the other metal objects, was an occupation of the pantry. Any kind of soft rag that had been boiled in milk and hartshorn powder (powdered stags' antlers) could be used to polish the silver and plated silver; whiting (sand-free chalk) moistened with ammonia, or alcohol, would remove spots of discolouration. In 1842 Needham's polishing paste came on the market, followed by a variety of other creams and liquids, Oakey and Globe both being household names.

Steel knives that were not in daily use – especially carving knives – were often rubbed with mutton fat and rolled up in brown paper to keep them from rusting. Before the invention of stainless steel, knives were washed and then polished using an abrasive such as emery powder or brick dust mixed with camphor and turpentine. Then along came rotary knife-cleaning machines, which could polish up to 12 blades at a time. The knives were placed in the slots at the top of the cylindrical wooden box containing buffers and bristles, which cleaned and polished both sides at the same time; an abrasive powder was poured through a chute.

'Rustless' steel was first manufactured in 1914; until modifications were introduced, stainless-steel knives, though easier to look after, were deficient in cutting power.

Top: Die-cut advertising give-away of a cabinet of knives, forks and spoons that unfolds to reveal its interior, c.1890.

Above: Kent was the best-known maker of Victorian knife-cleaning machines.

Above left: 1890s bill-head from G. W. Moses, general dealer of Dan's Castle, Co. Durham, advertising Needham's metal polish.

Above: Published by George Routledge in 1924, the book contains a selection from the 30,000 labour-saving hints and ideas submitted in a Good Housewife magazine competition.

Left: Advertisement of c.1900 for two of Oakey's household products, one showing a butler polishing knives in the pantry. Grates and the kitchen range had to be blackleaded.

HOT WATER AND BOILERS

Much domestic drudgery was removed at a stroke with the arrival of systems for providing running hot water in the kitchen. The chores of washing up, cleaning, scrubbing and laundering were immensely simplified as water no longer had to be heated on top of the stove, though some kitchen ranges did have a built-in tank and tap for hot water.

In the early 1900s individual gas geysers for fixing above the kitchen or scullery sink became available. These were copper cylinders linked to the water system, enabling hot water to be 'ready in 30 seconds', as the manufacturer Ewart & Son proclaimed. Their brochure from *c*.1910 pointed to the advantage hot water would be to the servants: 'To lessen their labours is half the battle. Do away with troublesome kitchen and copper fires.'

This system was largely overtaken by the installation of central boilers for hot water systems that ran throughout the house, and in rare cases fed radiators too. These were fuelled with coke or anthracite and, as advertisers pointed out, were also useful for warming the kitchen, burning up rubbish and airing clothes. They often included a hot plate for boiling a kettle for a cup of tea.

Above: Leaflet from the Gas Light & Coke Company, c.1910. Hot water made life for the servants considerably easier.

Left: 'Ewart's Geyser in the Scullery' from a brochure of c.1910. The appliance provided constant hot water, which was a novelty at the time.

Above: The Lightning model recommended for kitchen use by Ewart & Co., which guaranteed that gas fumes could not escape from the geyser.

Right and far right: Two advertisements from the May 1936 issue of the magazine The Ideal Home, one for the solid-fuelled Kokette boiler and the other for gas.

A minimum of Fuel—a maximum of Hot Water!

You'll be surprised how little fuel the KOKETTE requires in return for a bountiful supply of really hot water. Ample regulation too; will draw up quickly to heat the water with least delay, or can be closed down to a slow, prolonged smoulder. And the hot plate will always help you out when cooking and take a saucepan or two.

See about a KOKETTE to-day.

KOKETTE
THE BOILER YOU CAN DEPEND ON

Write to-day for an illustrated list or go and see the KOKETTE BOILERS at your local ironmongers

**T. BALMFORTH & CO., LTD.
LUTON.**
London: 36, Queen Street, E.C.4

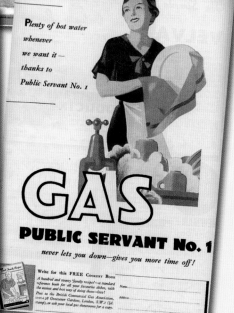

Plenty of hot water whenever we want it — thanks to Public Servant No. 1

GAS
PUBLIC SERVANT No. 1

never lets you down—gives you more time off!

Write for this FREE COOKERY BOOK

A hundred and twenty 'family recipes'—a standard reference book for all your favourite dishes, with the easiest and best way of doing them—free!
Post to the British Commercial Gas Association, Dept. 28 Grosvenor Gardens, London, S.W.1 (5d. stamp), or ask your local gas showroom for a copy.

Name ....
Address ....

LAUNDRY

Monday was wash day. Table linen would have been soaked overnight in cold water to lift stains, and candle wax and grease removed by adding soda to the water. To make the soap, a block of hard soap was shredded the previous day and added to water; resting the mixture on top of the stove turned it into a silky soft jelly. Proprietary soaps such as Lever Brothers' Sunlight and Lux came onto the market at the end of the 19th century.

Standing beside the tub, the maid twisted and turned the dolly energetically in the soapy water. The first washing-machines for use in the home appeared in the 1850s and were operated by turning a handle; later models incorporated a mangle. Tablecloths and napkins were 'blued', for whiteness, and starched, for stiffness.

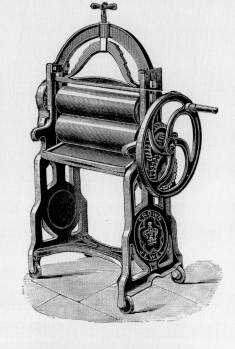

The washing was pegged to a line outside to dry, draped over a horse in the scullery or hung over the range. Sad irons were heated on the stove, and box irons had a cavity for a heated iron bolt or charcoal. From the 1880s it was possible to buy gas-heated irons, attached to the supply by a rubber tube, and by the 1920s forward-looking households possessed an electric iron.

Above and left: Victorian Crown Jewel Mangle with wooden rollers (top); wicker laundry basket (above); Edna iron (left) and Dalli hollow box iron with screen hand protector (far left), both heated with charcoal.

USE
Dr. Lovelace's Soap.

A
Familiar Scene in English Homes

SIDDONS'S SAD IRONS,
WITH IMPROVED CAST MALLEABLE IRON
HOLLOW HANDLES.

Handles much cooler when in use than any other kind.

Tops Japanned with a superior Enamel Black Varnish, and Faces very highly Polished.

MAY BE HAD HERE.

"BEACON"

16 in.
Rubber
Rollers.

Two
Years
Guarantee

WRINGER

A Premier quality wringer of superior finish,
of up-to-date design, yet of proved efficiency.

IN BLUE, RUST-PROOF
ENAMELS OF PLEASING
APPEARANCE

Will wring with ease the heaviest of blankets
—will not damage the flimsiest articles due
to the efficiency of the pure rubber Rollers
Constructed of best quality materials ; fitted
with Reversible Mangling Board, Cog Wheel
Guards and Drip Tray for catching all water.
COG WHEELS DIE CUT

*Above: Advertising leaflet for Dr Lovelace's Soap,
c.1900, with a dolly being used to tumble and stir
the washing in the soapy water.*

*Right: Mother's Help Gas Washing Machine, from
an 1890s leaflet. 'Will do the Fortnight's Wash for
a Family of Eight Persons in Two Hours.'*

*Above left: Early Victorian sad (meaning
'heavy') irons made of cast iron were heated
on the top of the range; they were also known
as flat irons.*

*Above: Leaflet advertising the Beacon
Wringer with rubber rollers, c.1930. It
stood over a tub, on top of a table or on
a special stand.*

WASHING UP

Soda and water, or soap made from soda combined with animal fat, had the strength to lift grease and soot from iron pots and pans. Bread and pastry boards and rolling pins were scrubbed with warm water and sand, and on no account were to come in contact with soda as it would be sucked into the wood and taint the food; nor should soda be used with aluminium. Stains were removed from enamelled wares with salt and sand; to give a shine to tin after washing it was rubbed with a paste of whiting and water, and polished with a leather; an oyster shell was kept in a kettle to prevent furring.

As well as having tired feet and an aching back from standing over the sink, the scullery-maid of Victorian times ended the day with hands that were red and raw from the soda. A thoughtful employer provided her with long-handled brushes and mops, and told her to treat her hands to a coating of glycerine.

Useful pieces of equipment recommended in 1929 by the author of *How to Own and Equip a House* were refuse holders, sink strainers, soap savers and 'a small device for cleaning the prongs of forks, consisting of strands of tow (flax fibre) stretching across a metal frame'.

Top: Blue-and-white plate, an advertising give-away for Hudson's Soap, c.1900. By grinding up a coarse bar of soap in his pharmacy in 1837, Robert Hudson invented dry soap powder.

Above: Decoration from the title page of the 1938 edition of Cookery for Every Household *by Florence B. Jack, 'for many years principal of the School of the Domestic Arts, Edinburgh.'*

THE "DOMESTIC" REFUSE HOLDER. *(cc)*

DOMESTIC Refuse Holder

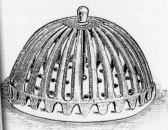

HUDSON'S
EXTRACT OF
SOAP
LEAVES NO SMELL

Wash up Dishes and Plates Forks, &c.
with HUDSON'S SOAP
Marvellous for Soaking and Washing Clothes

HAVE YOU TRIED THE PATENT
"LIAN" PAN SCRUBBER.

It is a Metal Sponge that will clean and scour pots, pans, dishes and tins better than anything. Can be instantly cleaned by plunging in boiling water. Will last a life-time. Nothing ever introduced so useful and

Above left: Sink strainers and refuse holders were among the items associated with washing up shown in catalogues of household goods in the 1920s.

Above: Hudson's Soap leaflet, c.1895. The soap extract was one of the most widely advertised products in Victorian and Edwardian times; one campaign involved balloons painted with the Hudson name.

Left: 'Will last a lifetime' was the claim for the metal sponge of c.1900 for cleaning and scouring cooking pots and pans and dishes.

ICE AND REFRIGERATORS

The arrival of the Wenham Lake Ice Company in the UK in the 1840s meant that a means of keeping food cold, in cities at least, was increasingly available: 'Ice is no longer a luxury confined to the splendid homes of the rich,' as one Victorian household book put it. Shipped across the Atlantic from New England in America, it was delivered to households in blocks from the company's London headquarters.

After struggling with feather pillows, sawdust or flannel as insulation, manufacturers devised the refrigerator, or ice closet – a zinc-lined wooden chest insulated with felt or asbestos that maintained a temperature low enough to prevent milk, meat and fish from going off, and was perfect for iced puddings. In 1893 Spong & Co.'s range, using ice blocks, varied from the 13in 'bachelor's' chest to the 50in cabinet refrigerator with provisions safe, wine cooler, iced-water tank and meat hooks.

Electrically powered domestic fridges were pioneered in America, manufactured by companies such as Frigidaire from the 1920s. Beyond the means of the average Briton, the advantages were clear: an enthusiast in 1932 recorded 'the benefit of putting a cold joint, salad, eggs, milk, stewed fruit, and custard in one, going away for a week-end or longer, and coming back to find it all ready to serve in perfect condition.'

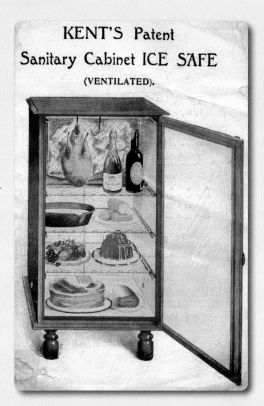

Above: A refrigerator 'faced with white odourless enamel that will neither crack, split or scale off', c.1910. Ice is packed into the back of the top shelf.

Left: Detail of a handbill advertising a Wenham Lake Ice Company refrigerator, c.1870. The company delivered ice in London at a cost of 1d per lb.

ELECTRIC REFRIGERATOR
Simplified Electric Refrigeration

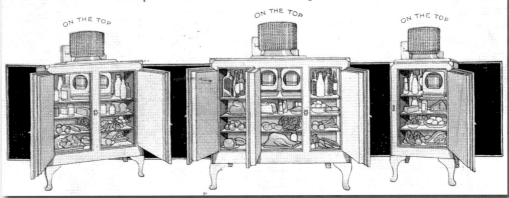

ON THE TOP   ON THE TOP   ON THE TOP

Above: 1936 advertisement for Zeros refrigerators. The happy housewife declares, 'When it came all I had to do was plug it in, just like a radio.'

Left: Electric refrigerators advertised in 1929. 'Install the B.T.H. Refrigerator and make it safe to be hungry in your own home.'

THE 20TH-CENTURY KITCHEN

As the housewife herself began to spend more time in her kitchen, so its design became more important. She aspired to 'The Perfect Kitchen' as a background to her domestic activities, with every convenience – the household budget could reasonably be spent on labour-saving equipment or a new-fangled Aga. Bright colour schemes and decorative touches such as rugs and curtains were introduced and, since some families were now eating breakfast there, and friends were dropping in for a cup of morning coffee, pretty tablecloths and cheerful china.

Walls and work surfaces might be covered in Vitrolite, an opaque glass material that could be ordered in turquoise, primrose, Wedgwood blue, shell-pink or orange. Like the enamel of the stove, it was a material that was easy to wipe clean. In a new house, the kitchen sink – now made of stainless steel – would be placed under the window, giving garden views denied to earlier inhabitants of the kitchen. A hatch through to the dining room made dishing up food simpler in the modern servantless age.

Tiled linoleum was popular on floors, and there might be a broom cupboard with space for a new vacuum cleaner. 'A pulley clothes airer fixed to the ceiling and a roller and brackets on which to hang a roller towel is a great convenience.'

You are looking through a kitchen-window at an Aga Cooker—the Country House Model. It never goes out from one end of the year to another, and withall burns fuel guaranteed to cost less than £5 a year. It has four ovens, two hot plates and a large simmering area.' There are 20,000 Agas in use to-day and models may be had from £35, or by hire purchase. Write for the catalogue.

AGA

Above: Advertisement for an Aga cooker from The Ideal Home, *1936: 'burns fuel guaranteed to cost less than £5 a year.'*

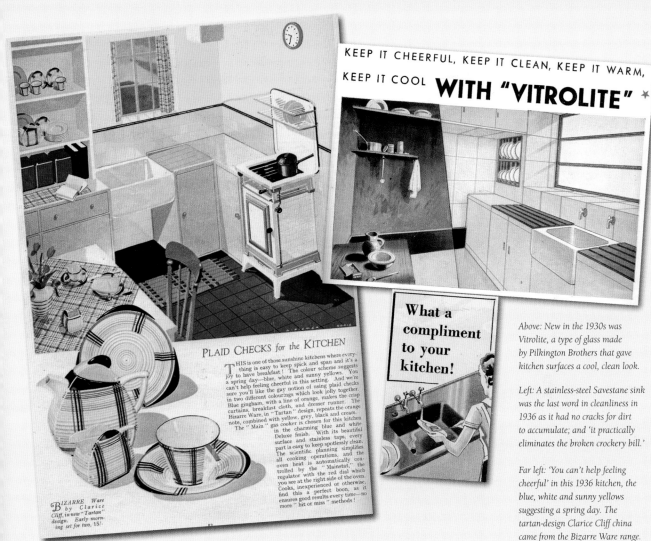

PLAID CHECKS for the KITCHEN

THIS is one of those sunshine kitchens where everything is easy to keep spick and span and it's a joy to have breakfast! The colour scheme suggests a spring day—blue, white and sunny yellows. You can't help feeling cheerful in this setting. And we're sure you'll like the gay notion of using plaid checks in two different colourings which look jolly together. Blue gingham, with a line of orange, makes the crisp curtains, breakfast cloth, and dresser runner. The Bizarre Ware, in "Tartan" design, repeats the orange note, combined with yellow, grey, black and cream.

The "Main" gas cooker is chosen for this kitchen in the charming blue and white Deluxe finish. With its beautiful surface and stainless taps, every part is easy to keep spotlessly clean. The scientific planning simplifies all cooking operations, and the oven heat is automatically controlled by the "Mainstat," the regulator with the red dial which you see at the right side of the oven. Cooks, inexperienced or otherwise, find this a perfect boon, as it ensures good results every time—no more "bit or miss" methods!

BIZARRE Ware by Clarice Cliff, in new "Tartan" design. Early morning set for two, 15/-.

What a compliment to your kitchen!

Above: New in the 1930s was Vitrolite, a type of glass made by Pilkington Brothers that gave kitchen surfaces a cool, clean look.

Left: A stainless-steel Savestane sink was the last word in cleanliness in 1936 as it had no cracks for dirt to accumulate; and 'it practically eliminates the broken crockery bill.'

Far left: 'You can't help feeling cheerful' in this 1936 kitchen, the blue, white and sunny yellows suggesting a spring day. The tartan-design Clarice Cliff china came from the Bizarre Ware range.

ELECTRIC COOKERS

As early as 1890 the General Electric Company sold a 'rapid cooking apparatus' that took 12 minutes to boil a pint of water. However, electricity was expensive and the supply slow to reach rural areas. In addition, early cookers were inefficient and badly designed, and they did not begin to make an impact on the market until the late 1920s.

'Switch-on Cookery' was the exciting phrase used in *The Way to a Good Table, Electric Cookery,* Elizabeth Craig's 1937 book published by the British Electrical Development Association in its determination to oust gas as the power of choice. The author listed the advantages: no flames, no matches, uniformly browned cakes and no blackened ceilings; 'Electricity is white, not black, magic'. Certainly, as families were increasingly eating and living in their kitchens, the appeal of cleanliness was convincing. Mrs Craig continued in proselytizing vein, 'If you are a housewife, you'll have more time to yourself. If you are a business woman, you simply can't do without one, in these days when time is money.'

A 1929 issue of *The Ideal Home* commended the Magnet range, whose exterior finish 'leaves nothing to be desired' and whose clear accompanying directions meant 'nothing could go wrong'. The Magnet Minor with single hotplate, grill and small oven was popular for people living in flats.

Above: This 1938 catalogue for aluminium pans stressed the fact that cooking with electricity had the advantages of absolute cleanliness and no fumes.

Above: The Electrical Development Association's logo of man in a pointed hat competed with the Gas Council's Mr Therm and did not survive long. Advertisement of 1936.

Right: The Reyrolle Connector made your cooker 'safe to handle'. Electric cookers used a higher wattage than people had been used to. Advertisement of 1929.

Above left: The silver cover, now tarnished, of Elizabeth Craig's 1937 book was clearly chosen to express the modernity of electricity.

Above: An illustration from The Way to a Good Table demonstrates how to clean the hob, 'the Main Switch having previously been turned OFF.'

PANS, PYREX AND POTS

With clean gas and electric cookers, heavy iron pans were very unsuitable. Enamel pans were commonly used, but the best material for them was considered to be aluminium, which was light, bright, strong and simple to clean. As one manufacturer pointed out, the thick base 'scientifically ground' to a dead flat surface made the pans perfect to use with an electric hotplate, and the new type of Bakelite handle was insulated and heat-resistant.

The appearance of oven-to-tableware was welcomed in the new servantless era when there were no longer cooks, parlourmaids and kitchen maids to dish up and wash up. Corning Glass of America manufactured a range of temperature-tolerant glass cookware, branded as Pyrex, in 1915; this was produced in Sunderland in England from 1922. Almost unbreakable, and decorative – there was a Blue Willow Pattern and a Cut Glass range – these casseroles and pie dishes sat perfectly on the new electric hotplates for keeping prepared food hot. As a 1938 advertisement proclaimed, 'Just 6d – all you need to start a Pyrex Collection'. Bourne & Son was one of the potteries that took advantage of this new trend, introducing both patterned Denby ovenproof wares and items with their Cottage Blue and Manor Green glazes.

Above and above right:
Aluminium ware: the Pyramid
Economy Steam Cooker consisting of
a pan and three steamers cost 43s 6d
and the Asparagus Boiler 30s 6d, from
the Pyramid 1938 catalogue.

Right: Denby Epic Casserole and Saucepan, economically priced
at 5s 11d and 4s 6d in a 1936 advertisement. They were described
as the 'ever popular service vessels for modern homes'.

"PYREX" BRAND

d of Oven · Regd Trade Mark · "PYREX" BRAND · For Every

makes you proud of your table

Sauce Boat. 1444 · 2/6
Small Sauce Boat. 1521 · 2/-
Sauce Boat Stand. 1464 · 1/9
Small Sauce Boat Stand. 1526 · 1/3

Soup Tureen. A504 · 2 pts. · 7/-
A506 · 2½ pts. · 9/9

Soup Ladle. 1504 Bowl: 2½" dia. 2/9

A BRIGHT IDEA !

ABRAIZO saves hours of scouring and cleaning. A brisk rub and your Aluminium ware shines like silver—all traces of stains, grease, burnt food, etc., disappearing like lightning—but it is for the ABRAIZO. Equally good for all other kitchen ware.

Look for ABRAIZO on every packet—lasts longer.

Tested and approved by GOOD HOUSEKEEPING INSTITUTE.

British Made.

ABRAIZO
THE ALUMINIUM CLEANER

7½d., 1/6 and 2/6.
Ironmongers, Grocers and Stores.
J. & A. McFARLANE, Ltd.,
Springbank Street,
Glasgow, N.W.

Introducing "PYREX" BRAND
Oven-table Glassware

Above: The modish cover of the 1938 catalogue of Pyramid Aluminium Utensils which, it was claimed, secured 'perfect cooking'.

Right: Wire-wool scourers such as Abraizo, which was recommended by the Good Housekeeping Institute, were the speedy answer to cleaning aluminium pans. Advertisement of 1933.

Top and above: 'For Every Kind of Oven, For Every Kind of Table'. A fold-out catalogue of the Pyrex range, 1938, which boasted that 'it has definitely been proved that food bakes more quickly and more thoroughly in "Pyrex" brand Ovenware'. The Round Streamline Casserole was priced at 5s 6d.

ELECTRICAL KITCHEN GADGETS

A 1920s Siemens brochure (distributed by the North Metropolitan Electric Power Supply Co., of High Barnet) summed up the new 'Modern Magic': 'No longer need Cooking, Ironing, Cleaning etc. be a never-ending round of tiresome tasks: with the aid of electricity leisure time lengthens and can be pleasurably spent – in Comfort – not, as is very often the case, resting from the fatigue of unassisted toil.' For the kitchen, the housewife could choose from the pages of the brochure electric irons, boiling rings, a milk or egg boiler, a warming plate, a kettle or a toaster. These of course could only be used in the household that had had electricity installed.

To calculate the cost of running appliances, the 1932 edition of *Electricity for Everybody* by R. Borlase Matthews had blank pages for noting down daily meter readings. He described new gadgets on the market, including an electric auto-grill for bacon and an electric coffee percolator for the popular new table cookery: 'manufacturers have carefully designed apparatus which provides a clean and convenient method of cooking light and tasty dishes on the breakfast or dining table.' Electric clocks, cake mixers, floor polishers, coffee-grinders, knife-cleaners, potato peelers, washing-machines and wringers were on his list, which in most households would have been a distant dream.

EVERYTHING ELECTRICAL

at the turn of any Switch

Above: From The Ideal Home *magazine of 1929, an advertisement for a Kohler Electric Plant that enabled electric kettles, toasters and irons to be at the ready day or night.*

THE ECONOMY OF THE SERVIS ELECTRIC WASHER (No. 1)

Mrs Young saves 3/- each week on her laundry Bill . . . .

MORE THAN SHE PAYS FOR HER SERVIS !

Even though she washed as many things at home as she could manage, Mrs. Young's laundry bill used to average 3/- a week. There she was, scrubbing and mangling and ironing every Monday—and she still had the laundryman to pay when Friday came round.

But that's all ended now. Her Servis Electric Washer does all her washing these days—Mrs. Young merely dumps the clothes in, switches on the current, and the "Servis" does the rest, leaving her free to attend to her household duties. It costs only ½d. an hour to run, and saves her 3/- each week. You simply must learn more about this wonderful washer. Why not post the coupon below for a free copy of the Servis illustrated folders.

or on convenient hire purchase terms. Also De Luxe, 18 gns., and Cabinet models, 24 gns

16 GNS.

ALL BRITISH

Servis
MADE IN ENGLAND

ELECTRIC WASHER

POST THIS COUPON TO-DAY

To Servis, 27, Grosvenor Place, S.W.1.   'Phone : Sloane 6795

Please send me a copy of the SERVIS Illustrated Folders.

Name ....

Address ....   (W.H. Nov.)

ATM MANUFACTURERS OF XCEL   *SIEMENS DISTRIBUTORS OF XCEL*

XCEL
ALL BRITISH

ELECTRIC DOMESTIC APPLIANCES

Modern Magic!

Above: In 1936 a Servis Electric Washer cost a farthing an hour to run but 16 guineas to buy, so most companies offered hire-purchase schemes.

Right: Handy electrical gadgets illustrated in Electricity for Everybody, *1932: a small immersion water heater, described as an Egg Boiler and Lifter for a single egg. The larger gadget was a device for grilling bacon 'perfectly and economically in three minutes.'*

Above: 1920s Siemens Xcel Electric Domestic Appliances were promoted as 'All British', since Siemens was originally a German company.

TRADESMEN

'Families waited on daily' is a phrase often found on old bills. When the mistress of the house went out herself to do the shopping, the goods would be delivered later to the back door. Chimney sweeps, knife-grinders, milkmen and laundrymen would also call here.

For the smooth running of the Victorian kitchen it was vital to use only tradesmen who could be trusted. Nonetheless, 'Hints for Housekeepers' in *Warne's Model Cookery and Housekeeping Book* remarked that 'Butchers' bills require careful weekly supervision, even when not paid till the quarter has elapsed, as errors in weight, even of ounces, or of price, as of farthings, come to a considerable item in the course of a year.'

Many shops still used the word 'merchant', thus 'Provision Merchant' and 'Wine and Spirit Merchant'; someone describing himself as an Italian Warehouseman stocked goods imported from Italy. If the kitchen was overstretched for a special event, made dishes would often be bought from Cook and Confectioners' shops. Suppliers invested in elegantly printed and illustrated trade cards, bill-heads and paper bags; often these featured a picture of a smart shop-front with customers' well-turned-out carriages lined up outside. Some, in particular grocers, gave out little leather-bound account books in which the weekly order could be noted and the cost totted up.

Above: Set of chromolithograph scraps of tradesmen, c.1880, showing a sweep, butcher, greengrocer and baker, each with their large delivery baskets.

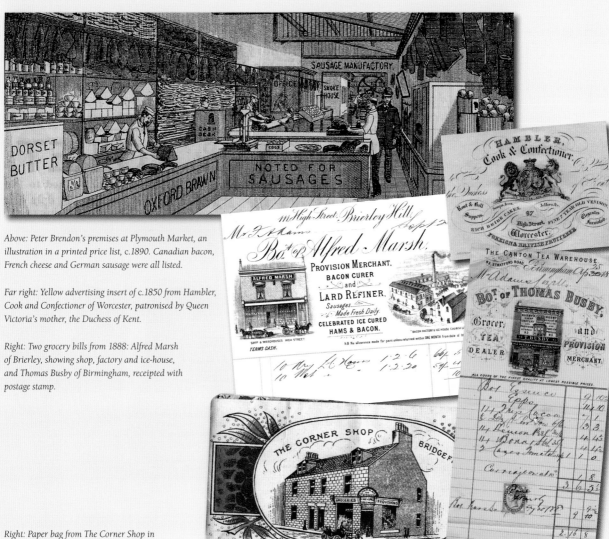

Above: Peter Brendon's premises at Plymouth Market, an illustration in a printed price list, c.1890. Canadian bacon, French cheese and German sausage were all listed.

Far right: Yellow advertising insert of c.1850 from Hambler, Cook and Confectioner of Worcester, patronised by Queen Victoria's mother, the Duchess of Kent.

Right: Two grocery bills from 1888: Alfred Marsh of Brierley, showing shop, factory and ice-house, and Thomas Busby of Birmingham, receipted with postage stamp.

Right: Paper bag from The Corner Shop in Bridgefield, c.1890, probably used for tea.

SHOPS AND SHOPPING

By the beginning of the 20th century, it was clear that ways of shopping were changing. The small specialist shopkeeper was being challenged by a group of highly competitive entrepreneurial grocers who saw that with numerous branches they could build up a reputation for quality and price, buy in bulk and promote cheaper own-label products. There was also a far wider range of packaged, tinned and bottled goods to sell. Food companies using new technologies proliferated; new foods were invented and, boosted by widespread advertising, many became household names. The patronage of famous cooks was sought: Francatelli recommended Crosse & Blackwell for macaroni, curry paste and vinegar, Robinson's patent groats for gruel, and Brown & Polson's patent cornflour for a soufflé pudding.

Typical of the new order were John & Mary Sainsbury, who in 1869 opened a shop selling fresh food in Drury Lane. By the time of John's death in 1928, there were 128 shops. Thomas Lipton's first shop was opened in 1871 in Glasgow, and by 1889 he had 30 branches in London and claimed to be 'the largest retail provision dealer in the world'. For poorer people, Co-operative Wholesale Society shops were a blessing since profit was returned to the shoppers in the form of dividends.

Above: Collection of three collectible cards put out by the Co-operative Wholesale Society in the 1920s promoting their own brands.

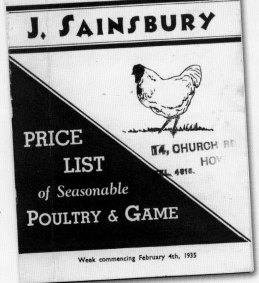

Above: Reverse of one of the cards shown opposite, printed with the Co-operative Wholesale Society (CWS) symbol of wheatsheaf, spade and sickle and their motto.

Above centre: Notebooks given away free by Home & Colonial Stores advertising its products on the inside covers. This one was used in 1926.

Right: Sainsbury's price list for February 1935 included a special offer of Surrey Fowls at 1s 4d per lb, and Plover and Capercailzie at 9d and 4s 6d each.

Above: Independent grocers, such as J. O. Jones of Colwyn Bay, submitted bills monthly on account. Mrs Howard spent £3 15s 6½d in March 1924.

BREAKFAST

A substantial breakfast to start the day was considered important, and it was the responsibility of the cook to offer variety. 'A nicely-laid, pretty, appetizing breakfast is a great promoter of good temper and harmony though the ensuing day,' was a typical injunction to the Victorian housewife. 'A soiled table-cloth, tough cold toast, weak tea, bitter coffee, Etc., are enough to derange both the temper and digestion of those who have to submit to such domestic inflictions.'

Help was to hand with such small volumes as *Breakfast Dishes for Every Morning of Three Months*. This suggested alternatives to the monotonous routine of boiled eggs, bacon, dried fish or sausages: for January 14th, Indian pillau, shrimp pie, pigs' trotters, muffins and stewed apples (pippins); and during the following week boiled hominy, bloaters and crumbs, snipe on toast, German dumplings and gravy, and potted calf's liver. Some dishes were acknowledged to be a touch too heavy for those with sedentary occupations, but excellent for those spending their days in the open air, riding, shooting, fishing or walking.

By the 1930s breakfasts had been slimmed down. For a busy household with less time to linger at the breakfast table, fresh grapefruit, orange juice and cereal, as well as toast and marmalade, featured on the menu.

Above: New-laid eggs and sausages, two die-cut advertising give-aways from The World's Tea company, c.1900.

Left: Toasting forks illustrated in the Victorian Cassell's Dictionary of Cookery.

Above: Chromolithograph trade card for Harris's Real Wiltshire Bacon, c.1900.

Left: Breakfast, for which Vita-Wheat was specially recommended by 'users' and the medical profession. Page from a give-away leaflet from Peek, Frean, c.1930.

Above: Nursery breakfast, an illustration from Elizabeth Craig's Cookery Illustrated and Household Management, 1936. 'Young children should have milk at every meal, fresh fruit and vegetables such as raw carrot.'

BREAD

The extent to which bread was a staple of the British household can be judged from an observation in a Victorian domestic manual dating from 1872, which states that the amount of bread needed per week for each servant was 8lb for a woman and 16lb for a man. This 'household' bread, made in most kitchens, was described in the same book as 'often bitter and unpalatable from a little want of care'. Contrasting in quality were the brioches, rolls, muffins and fancy breads, many of which contained butter, eggs and sugar, baked for the family's breakfast and afternoon tea. Careful cooks would buy their flour direct from the miller in an attempt to determine that it was not adulterated – a perennial problem. Also questionable, as well as the purity of the flour, was the nourishment value of shop-bought loaves.

Branded bread became a success as people came to trust the flour that was used. Hovis, which contained wheatgerm, had become a household name by 1895. It was sold as being healthy and more digestible than white bread; its slogan, 'Don't say brown, say Hovis,' was introduced in 1925. There were many imitators, among them Daren and Bermaline. The demanding silhouette of 1920s fashions heralded the beginning of the slimming industry and the innovation of crispbreads such as Ryvita and Vita-Wheat.

Above: Daren bread was made with flour milled in Dartford. The reverse of the advertising give-away of c.1900 claimed, 'if it were more in general use, there would be less indigestion and sufferings.'

Above: Bread Slicer in use in the early 20th century, one of the colourful illustrations from an enlarged edition of Mrs Beeton.

Right: An improvement on the toasting fork; the One Minute Toaster from the catalogue of Ramsay & Co.

Ber'maline Bread

THE PICK OF THE WHEAT FIELDS

of the world is drawn upon to produce BERMALINE BREAD. It appears on your breakfast table as a perfect food. Bermaline is rich in all those elements which make rich blood and strong bones. Those

of weak digestion thrive on it. In food value Bermaline ranks highest amongst all breads. It is a happy combination of all the vital elements of the purest wheat and Bermaline Malt extract.

Price List
FROM
THE MIDDLETON
FLOUR and GRAIN STORES
Family Millers.
113, DARTMOUTH PARK HILL
HIGHGATE, N.

All Orders to be sent to the ab
Address, where they will rec
prompt attention.

VANS TO ALL PARTS DAILY

Above: Montgomerie & Co. of Glasgow claimed it supplied Canadian wheat flour with 'special ingredients' to the agents for Bermaline bread, popular in the 1920s and 1930s.

Right: Price list, c.1890, from Middleton's, a family miller in Highgate, north London, supplying five grades of flour to local households.

A NEW FOOD
McVITA
(REGD)
Made entirely from English Wheat
by
McVITIE & PRICE
1/- PER PACKET

Price List
or
Flour. Meal, Grain. &c.

FLOUR.

				s.	d.
Whole Meal	10-½	½-pk. 9d.	pk.		
Best Household	10-½	" 9d.			
Pastry Whites	1/-	" 10d.			
Best Pastry Whites		" 11d.			
Self-Raising	1/1	" 1s.			

Please return all empty bags.

SCOTCH OATMEAL.
(Best Midlothian).

					s.	d.
Coarse	4d. per quart.	3½ lbs. 7½d.	7 lbs.		1	3
Medium	4d.	"	7½d.	"	1	3
Fine	4d.	"	7½d.	"	1	3

GRAIN.

		per peck.—s.	d.
Maize	- - -	1	0
Barley	- - -	1	0
Wheat	- - - 1s. &	1	2
Buckwheat	- - -	1	0
Dari	- - -	1	0
Fowls' Mixture	- - -	1	0
Pigeon "	- - 10d. &	1	0
Oats "	- - -	1	4
Barley Meal	7d., 9d. &	1	0
Middlings "	- - -	0	10
Bran "	- - -	0	6
	- - -	0	3

Above: Magazine advertisement for McVita, the 'new food', a slimming bread substitute. Full page of The Illustrated London News, May 4th 1935.

BREAKFAST CEREAL

Breakfast cereals were immigrants from America. Corn Flakes was invented almost accidentally by Dr John Harvey Kellogg, who was experimenting in 1876 with cooked wheat, trying to make it more appetizing for the patients at his health spa. The Battle Creek Toasted Corn Flake Company was founded by his brother Will Kellogg in 1902. By then, Henry Perky's Shredded Wheat and Charles William Post's Grape-Nuts were on the market in America.

It was not long before the cereals were rattling into breakfast bowls in England. Factories opened to meet the demand; in 1926 a factory made Shredded Wheat in Welwyn Garden City. Unlike the porridge that was so loved in Scotland, which needed to be stirred during the time it took to cook, these cereals required no preparation at all. They were deliciously crunchy, satisfying and, most appealing to the housewife providing for a family, nourishing. The makers advertised widely, extremely competitive in promoting the excellence of their brands: 'Mother Knows What's Best – In every packet of Kellogg's there are ten big platefuls of the finest Corn Flakes in the World.' It was the '30-second breakfast'. The makers of Quaker Oats – 'cooks in 5–10 minutes' – rushed to declare the benefits of porridge for a warming start to the day's work.

Above: 1940 advertisement for Shredded Wheat – 'one of the nicest, handiest, most economical breakfast foods you can buy' – emphasizing its value in building up strength in February, the month of low powers of resistance.

LITTLE JACK HORNER

Little Jack Horner, went 'round the corner
To buy himself something to eat.
"Here," said the grocer, "Kellogg's Corn
    Flakes, I know sir,
You'll consider a wonderful treat."

PETER, PETER, PUMPKIN EATER

Peter, Peter, Pumpkin Eater,
Had a wife and he *could* keep her.
He put Kellogg's Corn Flakes on the shelf,
So his wife could enjoy herself.

GET YOUR FUNNY JUNGLELAND BOOK

Simply fill in the coupon below with your name and address and send it to us with 3 tops from packets of Kellogg Cereals or 3d. in stamps. We will then send you an attractive Animal Booklet, made like this folder, and in full colors. Tear out and mail the coupon below.

KELLOGG COMPANY OF GREAT BRITAIN, LTD.,
Bush House, Aldwych,
London, W. C. 2.

I enclose { ———— 3 Kellogg Packet tops } for which please
{ ———— 3d. in stamps }
send me one of your Funny Jungleland Books.

Name...

"A FUNNY 'BISCUIT'!"

SHREDDED WHEAT

Above: Give-away leaflet with flaps that lift, an ingenious Kellogg's advertisement of 1933 designed to appeal to children, the principal consumers of Corn Flakes.

Right: Grape-nuts, made from wheat baked with malted barley, were the invention of the American Charles William Post. The claim of the 1937 advertisement was that they beat the 'fagged feeling'.

Above: Advertising insert of c.1905 for Shredded Wheat, the 'funny biscuit'. 'Get the Fibre in your Cereal food, and poor digestion and teeth will not trouble you.'

MILK

Victorian housekeeping manuals warned of the dangers of unwholesome milk – and with reason, since government inspections of 1877 revealed that one-quarter of all milk sold was seriously adulterated. Watering down was the most frequent offence and, when done from a dubious water supply, 'milk epidemics' – or worse, typhoid – often resulted from bacteria in the water. Thickening milk with starch and colouring it with egg yolk or saffron were other unscrupulous tricks. Boiling milk was recommended, particularly for children and invalids. Patent milk-boiling and sterilizing saucepans were therefore to be found in many kitchens: 'Cannot possibly boil over. Saves Milk, Time and Temper.'

The dairyman, or 'cowkeeper' as he sometimes described himself, carted churns to the door and ladled the milk directly into the household's own jug or bowl, which was then carried into the kitchen. The process was simplified by the introduction of delivery in glass bottles with porcelain stoppers by Express Dairies in the 1880s. Early sizes ranged from ⅛ to 2 pints. Well-founded fears of the dangers of unhygienic milk were lessened after pasteurisation was pioneered at the end of the 19th century, but many households preferred the safety of tinned milk, either evaporated or sweetened condensed, which became readily available in the same period and lasted indefinitely on the kitchen shelf.

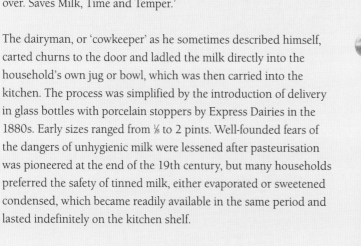

Above: Cardboard tops on milk bottles replaced porcelain stoppers; these in turn were replaced in the 1950s by aluminium foil.

Left: Chromolithograph scrap of a milkman pouring milk from churn to jug, c.1880. Milk bottled at a dairy was far more hygienic.

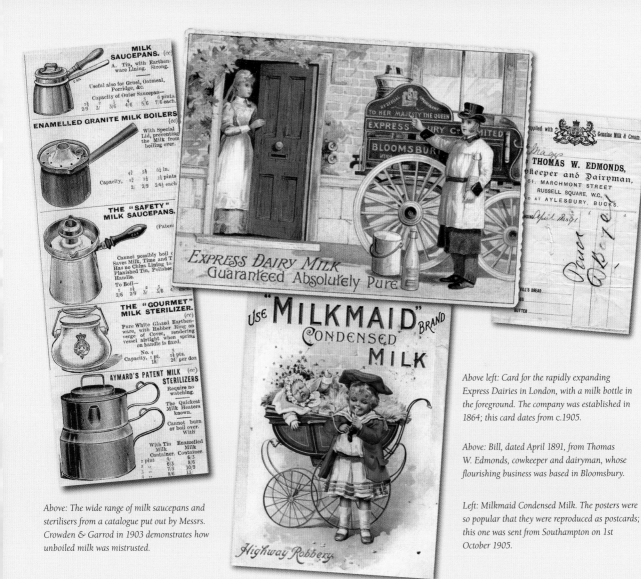

MILK SAUCEPANS. (cc)
A. Tin, with Earthenware Lining. Strong.

Useful also for Gruel, Oatmeal, Porridge, &c.
Capacity of Outer Saucepan—

ENAMELLED GRANITE MILK BOILERS (cc)
With Special Lid, preventing the Milk from boiling over.

Capacity,

THE "SAFETY" MILK SAUCEPANS.
(Patent

Cannot possibly boil
Saves Milk, Time and T
Has no China Lining to
Planished Tin, Polished
Handle.
To Boil—

THE "GOURMET" MILK STERILIZER. (cc)
Pure White Glazed Earthenware, with Rubber Ring on verge of Cover, rendering vessel airtight when spring on handle is fixed.
No. 4
Capacity, 1 pt.

AYMARD'S PATENT MILK STERILIZERS (cc)
Require no watching.
The Quickest Milk Heaters known.
Cannot burn or boil over.
With
With Tin | Enamelled
Container. | Container.

EXPRESS DAIRY MILK
Guaranteed Absolutely Pure

TO HER MAJESTY THE QUEEN
EXPRESS DAIRY CO LIMITED
BLOOMSBURY

Supplied with — *Genuine Milk & Cream.*

THOMAS W. EDMONDS,
Cowkeeper and Dairyman,
61, MARCHMONT STREET
RUSSELL SQUARE, W.C.
AND AT AYLESBURY, BUCKS.

USE **"MILKMAID"** BRAND
CONDENSED
MILK

Highway Robbery

Above: The wide range of milk saucepans and sterilisers from a catalogue put out by Messrs. Crowden & Garrod in 1903 demonstrates how unboiled milk was mistrusted.

Above left: Card for the rapidly expanding Express Dairies in London, with a milk bottle in the foreground. The company was established in 1864; this card dates from c.1905.

Above: Bill, dated April 1891, from Thomas W. Edmonds, cowkeeper and dairyman, whose flourishing business was based in Bloomsbury.

Left: Milkmaid Condensed Milk. The posters were so popular that they were reproduced as postcards; this one was sent from Southampton on 1st October 1905.

BUTTER AND MARGARINE

Late spring and summer was the best time for buttermaking. Cream was skimmed off the top of milk that had cooled in wide pans, either by hand or with a mechanical separator. It was then churned until the cream turned to golden butter, and a small amount of salt added to preserve it, though keeping butter from turning rancid was always problematic. The buttermilk was saved for making bread and scones. Butter made in the country and sold in towns was moulded into blocks with wooden pats and stamped with a design that identified the farm of origin. At the end of the 19th century salted butter arrived in refrigerated ships from Australia and New Zealand and elsewhere.

Editions of Mrs Beeton give instructions for curling butter for the table by twisting it in a cloth, 'so forming small and pretty little strings'; scooping butter into rolls with a spoon; and 'squirting' it through a paper cornet with holes in the bottom for garnishing hams, salads and eggs.

A cheap butter substitute, made from vegetable oils and named margarine, was invented by a French chemist. Manufacture began in the 1870s and it rapidly became one of the staples, with bread and jam, of the working-class diet. The success of chain grocers such as Maypole and Home & Colonial was based on the huge sales of margarine and its imitations such as Butterine and Buttapat.

Above: Engravings from Victorian catalogues: butter pats and prints used in butter-making at home, crockery, butter coolers and an implement for making butter curls for the table.

Above: Advertisement for the Diabolo Cream Separator, c.1900; the buttermilk is being poured into a pail, while the cream for butter is going into the pan.

Above: Advertisement issued by the Empire Marketing Board, c.1925, with an Irish Wolfhound indicating that the butter was from the Irish Free State.

Above right: Novelty advertisement from Home & Colonial for their margarine (the reverse is a Union Jack puzzle). 'Just like Butter' and 'Most Economical' were accompanying slogans.

Above: Buttapat, one of the butter substitutes on the market, an advertising postcard of c.1908.

COFFEE

The consumption of coffee declined in the Victorian period as tea became cheaper, and far more popular. A late 19th-century edition of Mrs Beeton states that the annual consumption of coffee per head of population was about 13oz, as against 6lb of tea. The recommended method of making coffee may not have encouraged the drinking of it: *The Cook's Dictionary*, in circulation in the early years of Victoria's reign, suggests boiling the coffee for an hour, noting that it would keep for up to five days in winter and could be reheated when needed. Not many years later this advice was contradicted.

Chicory, added for the sake of economy, imparted a slight bitterness to the coffee and darkened the colour. It was added to the coffee essences such as Mason's – 'fragrant and palatable' – that came onto the market in the 1880s. They were much used for giving a coffee flavour to ice creams and blancmanges. Coffee powder dates from the first decade of the 20th century but only became an 'instant' success with the arrival of Nescafé, which was launched in Switzerland in 1938. Nestlé was responding to the request to find some way of reducing Brazil's coffee surplus and making the drink more popular.

Above: Advertising give-away in the shape of Mason's Essence of Coffee with a recommendation from The Temple Magazine *on the back.*

Left: Electric coffee percolator illustrated in Electricity for Everybody, *1932. 'When provided with cold water and freshly ground coffee provides the most delightful cup of coffee imaginable.'*

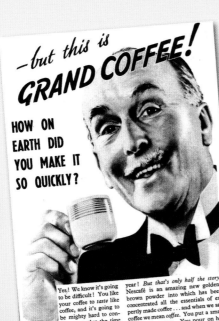

–but this is GRAND COFFEE!

HOW ON EARTH DID YOU MAKE IT SO QUICKLY?

Yes! We know it's going to be difficult! You like your coffee to *taste* like coffee, and it's going to be mighty hard to convince you that the time ... the window! ... arrived in ... you can now ... thousands ... inent every year! *But that's only half the story.* Nescafé is an amazing new golden-brown powder into which has been concentrated all the essentials of expertly made coffee ... and when we say coffee we mean *coffee*. You put a small spoonful in a cup. You pour on hot water. You prepare yourself for the most pleasant surprise of your life. And you get it! What flavour! What aroma! And to think — no grounds ... no waste ... and no more coffee po...

NESCAFÉ

Right: By 1939, when this advertisement was printed in Picture Post, *Nescafé had arrived in England: 'Real coffee – in a moment – in a cup!'*

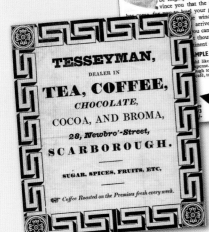

TESSEYMAN,
DEALER IN
TEA, COFFEE,
CHOCOLATE,
COCOA, AND BROMA,
28, Newbro'-Street,
SCARBOROUGH.

SUGAR, SPICES, FRUITS, ETC,

Coffee Roasted on the Premises fresh every week.

Left: Tesseyman of Scarborough roasted coffee beans on his premises in Scarborough every week. This label, possibly from the front of a paper bag, dates from c.1850.

THE OLD WAY & THE NEW.

MASON'S ESSENCE OF COFFEE.

MADE IN A MINUTE

MASON'S
HIGHLY RECOMMENDED BY THE
ESSENCE OF COFFEE AND CHICORY
DIRECTIONS
MANUFACTURED BY
NEWBALL & MASON
NOTTINGHAM.

THE FINEST COFFEE OBTAINABLE IS USED IN THIS EXTRACT.

Above: Advertising insert of c.1890 contrasting the old way of making coffee, which involved grinding the roasted beans, and the new easy way with coffee essence.

EGGS

The Victorian cook was adventurous in the matter of eggs. A cookery book describes plovers' and lapwings' eggs as 'much esteemed', and those of geese, ducks, turkeys and guinea fowls were also popular. To guarantee freshness, many families, even in towns, kept poultry in their back garden. Mrs Haweis wrote, 'They eat up all the worst scraps, take up very little room, and give hardly any trouble,' adding, 'and they amuse the cook.'

A recommended way to check whether eggs were fresh was to shake them, as they rattled when bad; if they lay obliquely when placed in a basin of water, they were not fresh, 'but may do for puddings etc.'; if, held up to the light, the shell showed small dark spots, 'they are very doubtful'; and probably completely rotten if there was no transparency in the shell. Eggs were the basis of many dishes, and winter shortages were a problem that was avoided by greasing the shells and storing them in a thick layer of bran or suspending them in buckets of isinglass (a form of gelatine).

Each period had its favourite egg recipe: the Victorians made Eggs à la Victoria – poached with truffles and puréed chicken – while in the early 20th century Omelette Arnold Bennett with cream, haddock and parmesan was fashionable.

Left and above left: Boiled egg in an eggcup, give-away advertisement for English eggs from The World's Stores, one of the smaller grocery chains that disappeared in the 1930s.

Above: Dishes from Warne's Model Cookery and Housekeeping Book of 1869: Plovers' Eggs (in a moss-lined basket) and Eggs à la Bonne Femme (stuffed with chopped beetroot and chicken).

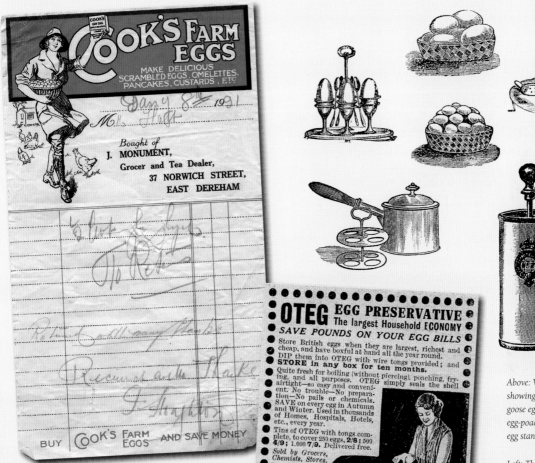

Above: Victorian engravings showing baskets of hen and goose eggs, two types of egg-poacher, a hard-boiled egg stand and an egg-beater.

Left: The relative scarcity of eggs in winter meant that even in 1936 products such as Oteg were sold, complete with tongs for dipping eggs into the preservative.

Above: The number of chicken farms expanded after the First World War and were often run by ex-servicemen. A 1921 bill-head advertising Cook's Farm Eggs in East Anglia, a traditional poultry-raising area.

LUNCHEON

Luncheon was regarded as of little consequence, a 'make-up meal, at which it is lawful to serve up half fowls and cut tarts,' according to *Cassell's Dictionary of Cookery*. The master of the house was at work during the week and his wife might take her luncheon with the children.

Hash was one of the most popular dishes – hashed chicken, game, rabbit, beef, mutton, whatever was left over from dinner the previous evening. Breadcrumbs, or flour, and gravy could be combined with the finely chopped meat and moulded into the shape of a cutlet or a heart for effect. Curries and toad-in-the-hole, which also made use of remnants, were often preferred to the monotony of cold cuts.

Puddings consisted of fruit pies, steamed puddings, junkets and jellies. In the 20th century cooks were advised to make up individual servings in the kitchen, doing away with serving dishes and saving on the washing up. Fruit and cheese and biscuits were often on the menu. A sweet luncheon cake, typically flavoured with nutmeg and lemon peel, made a good finale to this simple collation.

Above: 1. Cold Chickens 2. Lemon Pudding 3. Potatoes 4. Scalloped Veal 5. Salad 6. Honeycomb 7. Curried Eggs 8. Cutlets 9. Jam Tart. A luncheon menu illustrated in The Modern Householder: A Manual of Domestic Economy in All its Branches, *1872.*

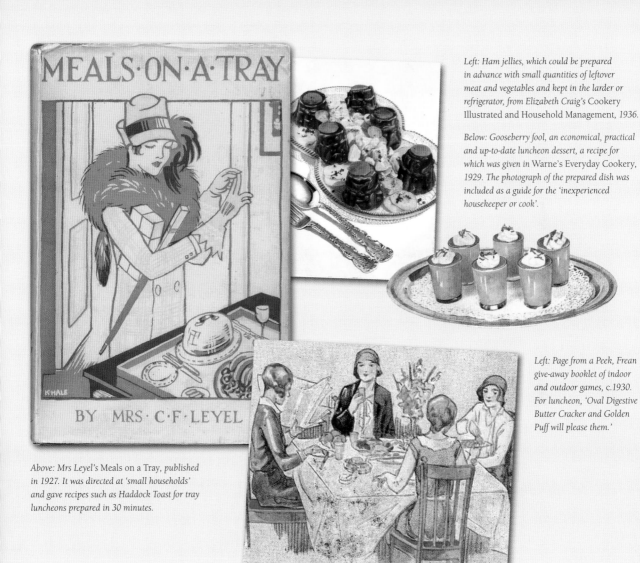

Left: Ham jellies, which could be prepared in advance with small quantities of leftover meat and vegetables and kept in the larder or refrigerator, from Elizabeth Craig's Cookery Illustrated and Household Management, *1936.*

Below: Gooseberry fool, an economical, practical and up-to-date luncheon dessert, a recipe for which was given in Warne's Everyday Cookery, *1929. The photograph of the prepared dish was included as a guide for the 'inexperienced housekeeper or cook'.*

Left: Page from a Peek, Frean give-away booklet of indoor and outdoor games, c.1930. For luncheon, 'Oval Digestive Butter Cracker and Golden Puff will please them.'

Above: Mrs Leyel's Meals on a Tray, *published in 1927. It was directed at 'small households' and gave recipes such as Haddock Toast for tray luncheons prepared in 30 minutes.*

POULTRY

J. C. Loudon, author of *The Suburban Gardener and Villa Companion* of 1855, reckoned that in any garden of over 50ft in length it was possible to have fowl-fattening houses, turkey houses and pigeon houses; keeping pigeons in a small garden was controversial, however, since little could be done to prevent them fattening at the expense of the neighbours' kitchen gardens.

'Well-fattened and tender, a fowl is to the cook what the canvas is to the painter,' was an observation in the 1869 edition of Mrs Beeton; 'do we not see it served boiled, roasted, fried, fricasseed, hashed, hot, cold, whole, dismembered, boned, broiled, stuffed on dishes, and in pies, – always handy and ever acceptable.'

'White-legged fowls and chickens should be chosen for boiling because their appearance is the most delicate when dressed,' wrote Eliza Acton in the 1840s; 'but the dark-legged ones often prove more juicy and of better flavour when roasted, and their colour then is immaterial.'

Top: Boiled Capon with Velouté Sauce, with 'a piece of slitted fat bacon' on the breast, from Mrs A. B. Marshall's Cookery Book, 1897.

Above: Chaudfroid of Chicken, on a bed of salad and garnished with chopped aspic, from Warne's Everyday Cookery, 1929.

The recipe for French Chicken Cutlets was a useful one for leftovers; cutlet-shaped pieces being dipped in beaten egg and coated with breadcrumbs. To smarten up the dish, they might be arranged around a mushroom purée and garnished with heart-shaped croutons, an inexpensive idea from Mrs Craig in 1936.

Left: Die-cut scrap of a poulterer, c.1880.

Roast Turkey.

Boiled Fowl.

Boned Capon.

Roast Goose

Roast Duck.

Roast

Menu

Clear Soup.

Cold Salmon
Cutlets,
Horseradish Sauce.

Chicken Croquettes.

Saddle of Lamb.
Potatoes.
Green Peas.

Lemon Cheesecakes.
Compôte of Fruit.

Cheese Straws.

Above: Poultry from an illustration in an 1893 edition of Mrs Beeton. A sage-and-onion stuffing was recommended for roast goose, and apple sauce. Goose was acknowledged to be a 'troublesome' bird to carve.

Left: Keevil and Keevil's label of c.1910 for poultry, game and meat sold at the London Central Market.

Right: Menu from an 1893 edition of Mrs Beeton for six to twelve persons in July which included Chicken Croquettes.

ESTABLISHED IN OLD NEWGATE MARKET 1797.

KEEVIL AND **KEEVIL**

POULTRY, GAME & MEAT SALESMEN,

Telephones: City 5096 & 5097.

228, 229, 230 & 231
LONDON CENTRAL MARKET

GAME

'There is no article of food that is so deceiving in appearance to know if it is young, tender, and good, or not, as game,' wrote Soyer in *The Modern Housewife*. 'Young birds may be distinguished by the softness of their quills ... Old pheasants are known by the length and sharpness of their spurs, in young ones they are short and blunt. Old partridges before Christmas have light blue legs, instead of yellow-brown. Wild fowl may be known to be old from their bills and the stiffness of the sinews of the legs, those that have the finest plumage are the worst eating.' The birds were labelled with the date on which they were received into the household, and hung to tenderise the meat and allow a strong, gamey flavour to develop.

Old rabbit was fit only for soup and old hare for soup or jugging – the blood and pounded liver, and forcemeat balls made with the heart and kidneys, stewed with the pieces of meat; port and redcurrant jelly were added just before sending to table.

Cold game pies were sometimes sent as presents at Christmas time. On the menu for Queen Victoria's dinner on Christmas Day 1899 were woodcock pie and game pie.

Above: Pheasant, Hare, Black Cock and a variety of game dishes, including Game Pie with Jelly and Macaroni Timbale and Rabbit, illustrated in an 1893 edition of Mrs Beeton.

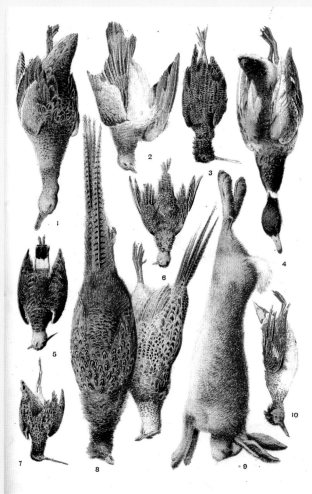

1.—Hen Wild Duck. 2.—Wood Pigeon. 3.—Woodcock. 4.—Cock Wild Duck.
5.—Black Plover. 6.—Golden Plover.
7.—Snipe. 8.—Pheasants. 9.—Hare.
10.—Teal.

Left: Game, such as hare and various types of wild bird, were hung for several days before they were ready to be cooked. Illustration from a 1903 edition of Mrs Beeton.

Below: Bill dated 1890 from E. E. Hankin, a 'Licensed Dealer in Game' in Hitchen. Hankin was also a poulterer, fishmonger and ice merchant.

Below: Pilau of Quails, a recipe in Mrs A. B. Marshall's Cookery Book allowing 'one bird and about an ounce of fat and lean bacon to each person.'

CHEESE

'Old cheese, taken in small quantities, after dinner, is an excellent *digester*, by causing chemical changes among the particles of food previously eaten.' This was the view held in the mid-19th century by J. Timbs in his *Hints for the Table* published in 1859. Very ripe cheese was savoured, and there were instructions as to how Stilton could be brought to perfection by scooping blue mould from an old cheese into a new one.

'To keep moist a piece of cheese in daily use, when it comes from the table wrap it at once in a damp cloth, preferably damped with beer, and keep it in a nearly airtight tin,' was the advice given in a 1903 edition of Mrs Beeton. This has a colour chart identifying 20 popular cheeses of the period (including one called, mysteriously, 'Koboko'). Of the cheeses illustrated only nine were British; it was not surprising, then, that the government should run a campaign to eat more English cheese during the depressed years of the 1930s, when it was promoted as one of the cheapest and best foods that could be bought, 'for it builds bones and muscles and helps us keep fit.'

Processed cheese came from America. James L. Kraft patented the manufacturing technique in 1916, and circular boxes of foil-wrapped triangles soon appeared in British larders.

1—Gorgonzola. 2—Double Gloucester. 3—Koboko. 4—Parmesan. 5—Dutch. 6—Roquefort. 7—Schabzieger. 8—Dunragit. 9—York Cream. 10—Port du Salut. 11—Cheddar. 12—Pommel. 13—Camembert. 14—Mainzer. 15—Cheshire. 16—Stilton. 17—Cream Bondon. 18—Gruyère. 19—Wiltshire Loaf. 20—Cheddar Loaf.

Above: Twenty types of cheese from a 1903 edition of Mrs Beeton. She recommended cheese be served on a folded napkin accompanied by butter and biscuits.

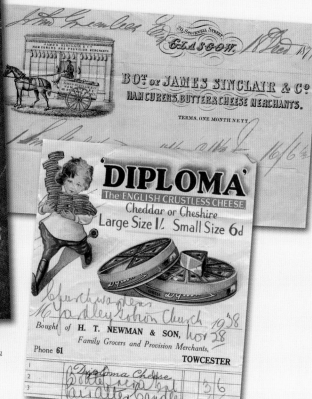

Left: Leaflet issued by the National Milk Publicity Council, c.1930. 'If you eat English cheese you are giving employment to a large number of people.'

Below: Bill-head from the Glasgow shopkeeper James Sinclair, dated 1871. Typically, at this period, a grocer might sell only butter, cheese, ham and bacon.

Right: English Diploma processed cheese advertised on a bill-head from the grocer H. T. Newman of Towcester in 1928. With no inedible rind, this 'crustless' cheese was perceived as good value for money.

SALT, SPICES AND MUSTARD

Salt for preserving and flavouring was bought in coarse blocks and often stored in a wooden box near the stove to keep dry. In 1894 a chemist, George Weddell, made the important discovery that the addition of calcium and magnesium made salt free-flowing. He founded Cerebos and his 'table' salt was an immediate success; he gave away salt cellars and spoons in return for coupons packed in the boxes. Saxa was introduced as a brand in 1907 for small boxes of salt.

Because of the long historical links of Britain with India, curries, kedgeree and mulligatawny soup, as well as chutney, had a place on the British table. Spices such as fenugreek, turmeric, cayenne pepper, ginger, coriander, cumin and cardamoms were available from some chemists. Cloves, cinnamon and nutmeg, which were used in puddings, were to be found in most store cupboards.

Mustard was an ingredient of traditional recipes for devilled kidneys, cauliflower cheese and Welsh rarebit. It was almost synonymous with the name Colman. The Norfolk family firm adopted the bull's head trademark in 1856 and ten years later was granted the Royal Warrant by Queen Victoria. The expression 'as keen as mustard' is often thought to come from the name of another mustard manufacturer, Keen & Sons, which was bought by Colman's in 1903.

Left: Victorian die-cut give-away featuring a sandwich-man advertising Keen's mustard. It opens out as a calendar for 1892. The company was established in George II's reign in 1742 and had a scallop shell trademark.

Below: In their advertisements – as in this one of c.1900 – Cerebos made frequent use of the old English proverb that children could catch a bird by putting salt on its tail.

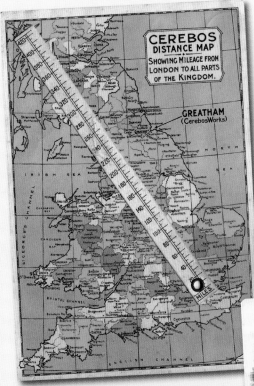

Above: Novelty give-away of c.1920 from Cerebos, 'Pure, Wholesome and Beneficial'; the ruler pivots from London on the map of Britain to measure mileage.

Above right: Advertising card of 1889 extolling the quality of Colman's mustard, which was originally sold as a powder.

Above: By 1917 Colman's were describing themselves as 'the largest mustard manufacturers in the world'. They also made starch and blue for the laundry.

Above: Victorian label for double refined table salt manufactured by J. Brough & Co. of Liverpool; nearby Northwich was the centre of the British salt industry.

VEGETABLES

Where there was a kitchen garden, an abundant supply of fresh vegetables of the season could be expected. Victorian seed catalogues display a wide variety, from the unusual such as rampion, salsify and cardoons, to the ordinary. Root vegetables were stored in layers of dry sand, and marrows, cabbages and onion kept well on cold stone floors. Peas, beans and cauliflowers were salted. For those dependent on bought vegetables there was less choice: an author on nutrition wrote in 1876 that 'potatoes, cabbages, onion, carrots and turnips, with a few more, express the extreme limits of all that the ordinary greengrocer desires to offer his customers for selection; the rest are luxuries.'

Vegetables were more often used as garnishing than as accompaniments to food; recipes generally involved lengthy boiling – for a purée of carrots simmer for two hours and for a cabbage half-an-hour. A determined band formed the Vegetarian Society in 1847, and by 1903 Mrs Beeton was including recipes for vegetarian households such as Mock White Fish made with salsify and Vegetable Goose (onion, parsley and breadcrumbs baked and cut into squares). It appears that salad was not then taken seriously unless it was based on chicken, lobster or decoratively set in aspic; at the very least it must include hard-boiled egg to render it worthwhile.

Above: Victorian scrap of a costermonger plying his trade from his donkey cart c.1880. Many households would have bought vegetables from street sellers.

Left: French Vegetable Cutter, a contrivance for cutting carrots and turnips into various shapes for 'soups, haricots, garnishing, etc.,' from Warne's Model Cookery and Housekeeping Book, 1869.

Above left: Selection of salads from Mrs Beeton, who wrote that 'whatever their composition, they should look cool, inviting, and dainty.'

Above centre: Vegetables presented in an edition of Mrs Beeton. For green vegetables, she recommended adding soda to the boiling water to preserve their colour.

Above right: The convenience of Heinz Salad Cream poured straight from the bottle onto salad made it the dressing of choice in the interwar years. Advertisement of 1935.

Above: Carters seed packet dating from c.1920 for growing a basic range of vegetables. The company was By Appointment to Queen Victoria.

SAUCES AND PICKLES

The British passion for enlivening cold meat, grilled chops and the like with a dash of piquant sauce or relish, or a dab of sour-sweet pickle, was a boon to the Victorian food manufacturer. Although recipe books were not short of home-made versions such as Quin's Sauce (two wineglassfuls of port and two of walnut pickle, four of mushroom ketchup, half-a-dozen anchovies pounded and the same number of eschalots, a tablespoonful of soy and half a drachm of cayenne pepper), there were numerous commercial brands jostling for a place in the store cupboard. Many of the sauces were named after their place of origin – Worcester, Yorkshire, Herefordshire and Warwickshire. Their ingredients were unlisted and secret. Labels typically included the word 'finest' and proclaimed that they were the perfect addition to 'gravies, curries, game, fish, rump steak, roast meat, cutlets, soups, etc.' Ketchups, or catsups, spicy sauces made from a single ingredient such as mushrooms, walnuts and tomatoes, were also popular.

Onions, beetroot, red cabbage and cauliflower were the easiest to pickle at home, sometimes combined to make piccalilli. Warnings were issued on the danger of doing this in copper pans, since vinegar would react with the metal and poison the produce.

Above: Edwardian advertising scraps for Farrow's Mushroom Ketchup and Fletcher's Tomato Sauce. A recipe for home-made mushroom ketchup included allspice, ginger, cayenne pepper, mace and brandy.

Right: Yorkshire Relish manufactured in Leeds, an advertisement of c.1880. In a competitive marketplace, superlatives such as largest, best and millions were used with freedom.

Above centre: Label for Herefordshire Sauce, c.1850, made on a small local scale in Ross-on-Wye 'from a recipe of a gentleman in the neighbourhood.'

Far right: Seed packet of c.1910 for red cabbage, grown for pickling. The pickle was simply made by salting the vegetable then covering it in boiling vinegar with peppercorns.

Right: London-made Mandarin Sauce used a Chinaman trademark and the humorous slogan 'Sauce for the Goose is Sauce for the Gander,' c.1890.

Far right: Advertising postcard for vinegar, 1908. The sender was telling a friend of her impending marriage and wrote, 'excuse p.c. the only one I have handy.'

PASTRY

The reputation of many a cook has rested on her having a light hand with pastry – a significant skill since pies and tarts of all descriptions have always been favourites on the British table. Smooth, cold hands were then held to be the secret, and the Victorian cookery writer Mary Jewry suggested that in hot weather the cook should plunge her hands into cold water before starting.

Pastry for that *pièce de résistance*, the raised pie, was frequently inedible since it was merely a decorative moulded case for the meats and juices, while pastry for 'common pies' was made with flour and dripping (mutton fat was generally avoided as too disgusting) or suet. *Cassell's Dictionary of Cookery* compared this cheaper kind to a rich cream pastry for tarts using 1lb of butter to 1lb of flour, plus sugar and cream, costing 1s 6d per lb to make.

By the 1930s creamed cooking fats, such as Spry, were on the market, the claim being that their light 'melt in the mouth' pastry was now foolproof, a quality simultaneously attributed to the reliability of the electric cooker at this time. Dependable flour was crucial; companies such as McDougall's handed out little recipe books to boost loyalty.

Above: Line engravings from Victorian cookery books showing equipment useful in pastry-making, including pie tins and an implement for cutting pastry at right angles.

Left: The Cookery Lesson, *a give-away advertising calendar bookmark for McDougall's flour, 1896.*

Right: The 1935 booklet Christmas Cheer included recipes for tarts and a five-page guide to icing a cake to make 'a dream of festive perfection'.

Far right: 1920s card advertising Federation Flour, the Co-op's own brand. Self-raising flour, with chemical leavening already added, was introduced generally from the 1880s.

Below: One way to boost sales was to give away recipes. McDougall's were at the forefront; their Handy Cookery Book, a leaflet with basic recipes, dates from c.1900.

18

MISCELLANEOUS.

SHORT CRUST PASTRY.

¼-lb. **McDougall's Self-Raising Flour,** ¼ teaspoonful Salt, 3-ozs. Dripping, Lard, or Butter. Cold Water to mix.

Put the flour and salt in a basin, rub in the dripping and mix to a stiff paste with water. Roll out, and bake at once in a quick oven.

NOTE.—This paste may be used for Meat Pie, Fruit Tart, Sausage Rolls, Meat Patties, etc., etc.

If a richer paste is required an extra ounce of dripping can be added.

19

SYRUP TART.

Trimmings of Short Crust Pastry. Equal quantities of Golden Syrup and Bread Crumbs.

Roll out the paste and cover a greased plate with it. Mix the golden syrup and bread crumbs, spread the mixture over paste, lay strips of paste across, and bake in a quick oven for twenty minutes.

NOTE.—Jam may be used in place of Syrup.

PIES AND TARTS

'A pie of young rooks is tolerable, it is the best form of using these birds as food,' stated one Victorian kitchen authority. What is certain is that the British passion for putting a pastry lid on almost any foodstuff extended to conger-eel, sole with oysters, herrings, lobster, calf's head, lambs' tongues, giblets, larks, sparrows and plovers with rumpsteak and hard-boiled egg, let alone more prosaic choices such as rabbit, game, and steak and kidney. Almost every region of the British Isles had a pie to its name: Devonshire squab; Cheshire pork; Shropshire bacon, artichoke and rabbit.

Pastry was hard to cook with a coal range, and one set of instructions suggests that if you could put your hand in the oven for more than a few seconds it would be too cold and the resulting food heavy with a dull look. Temperature-controlled gas and electric cookers gave the cook the confidence to embark on making vol-au-vents, lemon meringue pies and jam puffs.

Pies and tarts made with rhubarb, blackberries, apple, gooseberries and cherries were always among the nation's favourite home-made puddings, a fact exploited by J. Lyons & Co., whose 2d individual fruit pies were one of their most successful products.

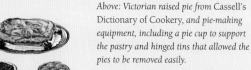

Above: Victorian raised pie from Cassell's Dictionary of Cookery, *and pie-making equipment, including a pie cup to support the pastry and hinged tins that allowed the pies to be removed easily.*

Left: Beefsteak pie, fruit flans and apple pie, illustrations from Warne's Everyday Cookery, *1929, of favourite dishes of the period.*

Right: Individually boxed and costing 2d each, Lyons Individual Fruit Pies were made with fillings that included peach, pineapple and raspberry. Illustration from a Lyons cake catalogue of 1938.

Below: Leaflet of recipes put out by Radiation, manufacturers of gas cookers, c.1935: 'Small fruit pies regulo setting mark 7, time 25 minutes.'

Left: Pies from Warne's Model Cookery and Housekeeping Book of 1869. In the centre is a raised Christmas game pie.

PUDDINGS

Boiled plum pudding (along with roast beef) was considered the quintessential British dish; *Cassell's Dictionary of Cookery* gave 12 different recipes, from Cottage, through Economical to Plain, Family and Excellent. They contained varying amounts of beef or mutton suet, currants, eggs, sugar, brandy and spices. The outside of Hedgehog Plum Pudding was spiked all over with almonds.

Famous persons and institutions had puddings named after them – Albert, Victoria, Duke of Portland and Brasenose College; other names were Cabinet and Military. Fillings might include apples, lemons, raisins and breadcrumbs. The puddings were boiled for several hours, either in a mould or wrapped in a cloth; 'large puddings are sometimes tethered to the ring of a twelve-pound weight to keep them below water in the pot.'

Lighter, baked milk puddings using ingredients such as rice, sago, tapioca or semolina gradually took over in popularity. This reflected the less robust eating habits of the 20th century, and the fact that cooking them was far more economical in fuel. 'Pudding' had by now become the word commonly used for a sweet or dessert.

Agnes Jekyll in 1922 was firm in her opinion that among the best hot puddings were Baked Jam Roly-Poly and Bread-and-Butter Pudding. They were especially suitable for what she termed 'cottage hospitality', at a midday meal or a simple supper.

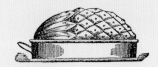

Top: Victorian enthusiasm for decorative shapes extended to moulds for boiled puddings including, in this selection from Mrs Beeton, 1893, one in the shape of a pineapple.

Above: Leaflet for The Queen's Pudding Boiler. Puddings such as roly-polys were either wrapped in cloth and placed in boiling water or the ingredients were boiled in a basin or mould covered in a cloth.

Marbled Jelly.

Blanc-Mange.

Trifle.

Almond Puddings.

Rout Cakes.

Jam Pudding.

Tartlets.

Mince Pies.

Vanilla Cream.

Apple Marmalade Tart

Cherry Tart

Pear & Apple Dumplings.

Charlotte Russe.

Dessert Biscuits.

Gingerbread Pudd

Fruit Tart.

Milk Pudding

Christmas Plum Pudding.

Apples & Rice.

Pancakes.

Left: Sweets from an 1893 edition of Mrs Beeton, including a gingerbread pudding, Christmas pudding and small individual almond puddings.

Below: A useful shortcut for puddings, Birds's Egg Powder, one of chemist Alfred Bird's range of culinary products introduced from 1855 onwards. Advertisement of c.1900.

THIS IS THE PUDDING MADE EVERY MORN, BY THE CLEVER MAIDEN ALL FORLORN THAT MILKED THE COW WITH THE CRUMPLED HORN THAT TOSSED THE DOG, THAT WORRIED THE CAT THAT KILLED THE RAT, THAT ATE THE MALT THAT LAY IN THE HOUSE THAT JACK BUILT.

THIS IS THE PACKET EACH HOUSE SHOULD ADORN THAT PUDDINGS WERE MADE WITH EVERY MORN. BY THE CLEVER MAIDEN ALL FORLORN THAT MILKED THE COW WITH THE CRUMPLED HORN THAT TOSSED THE DOG, THAT WORRIED THE CAT, THAT KILLED THE RAT, THAT ATE THE MALT THAT LAY IN THE HOUSE THAT JACK BUILT.

THIS IS THE COCK THAT CROWED IN THE MORN, WHO BECAME SO DEPRESSED HE REFUSED HIS CORN AND WISHED HIS CHICKS HAD NEVER BEEN BORN, NOW THAT EGGS ARE TREATED WITH SCORN

THE CLEVER YOUNG MAIDEN ALL FORLORN WANTS NO MORE EGGS ALLOWED HER AND PROCLAIMS ALL DAY WITH TRUMPET & HORN SHE USES BIRD'S EGG POWDER.

FRUIT

An ornamental centrepiece overflowing with carefully arranged fruit, or a dish decoratively filled with, for example, crystallised redcurrants stuck into a mossy mound, was often the focal point of a dining table. Fruit was offered as a dessert and eaten off specially elegant china using knives with silver rather than steel blades.

Fruit was 'generally more wholesome at luncheon than in any other part of the day', since there was a nervousness in the 19th century about the effect of raw fruit on the digestion: 'the skin of the gooseberry being very indigestible is never swallowed.'

Producing pineapples, melons, peaches and grapes from hothouses was a matter of pride for many a grand household; the average Briton was introduced to exotic fruit as fast steam ships began arriving at ports laden with pineapples from the West Indies, bananas from the Canary Islands (first imported by E. W. Fyffe in 1888), lemons from Sicily and the oranges that became particularly associated with Christmas from Spain and Portugal.

Recipes for cooking with native apples, pears, plums and cherries were legion: jams, jellies, jumbles, preserves, compotes, charlottes, creams, tarts, pies, puddings, fritters, ices, fools, soufflés, vinegars and syrups. Pears and apples that were 'keepers' – such as Norfolk biffins – were laid in racks; soft fruit was bottled, a task facilitated by the invention of the Kilner jar, manufactured from 1842.

These two economical dishes are universal favourites.

BANANA CHARTREUSE.
Line a fluted jelly mould, with a pipe in the centre, with a layer of Wine Jelly, and decorate the bottom with halves of glacé cherries and slices of bananas; cover this with a layer of jelly, and when set, or nearly so, put another layer of banana slices, and continue this till the mould is completely filled. To set this well, the mould should be placed in a pan and surrounded with crushed ice. When firm, dip the mould in tepid water for a few seconds and unmould the shape on to a cold dish. Fill the centre with stiffly whipped cream slightly sweetened, or some vanilla custard. Serve.

This one particularly appeals to the children.

FAMILY BANANA PUDDING.
Butter some slices of thin bread and place in a buttered pie-dish. Cut some bananas in half lengthways, and fill the dish alternately with bread and banana; beat two eggs well, add two tablespoonfuls of sugar, and grate a little nutmeg into it. Stir it gently into a pint of boiling milk, then pour into the pie-dish, and bake for ten minutes.

Above: Advertisment of c.1900 for West Indian Bananas. When opened out, it gives two banana recipes: Banana Chartreuse and Family Banana Pudding.

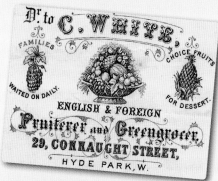

Above: Silver table centrepieces showing arrangements of fruit for dessert from The Modern Householder, 1872: 'the beauty of the fruit may be enhanced by surrounding it with foliage.'

Left: Trade card from the 1890s from C. White, Fruiterer and Greengrocer in the West End of London who specialised in 'choice fruits for dessert'.

Left and below: Survivals from the 1920s: original individual tissue wrappers for imported Spanish and Sicilian citrus fruit, one of which was destined for the Christmas market with an image of Santa Claus.

PRESERVES

If it was not to be bottled, summer fruit was often preserved 'dry', or candied, which was best done with greengages, apricots, nectarines, peaches and cherries. These were steeped in boiling sugar syrup on three to five successive days, and then allowed to dry before being carefully laid between sheets of paper and stored in a cool place. Quince and damson cheese were made by boiling the fruit until it became a stiff paste.

The alternative was to make jam or jelly. Those made from soft fruits such as strawberries and raspberries were the most prized, but a workaday jam was made with contributions from the vegetable patch: carrots (to make imitation apricot jam), beetroot, marrow (made more palatable with the addition of whisky and ginger) and pumpkin. 'Marmalade' was a word often used not only for a jam made with oranges and lemons but also with harder fruits such as quinces and pineapples.

However, home-made jam, and particularly marmalade, often compared badly with the cost of shop-bought jam, so the jam-making industry thrived. Companies such as Keiller's of Dundee, credited with being the first to turn bitter Seville oranges into a preserve, Chivers, a firm of East Anglian farmers, and Robertson's – James, the founder, was a Paisley grocer – were among many competing for a market share.

Above: Surreal 1898 advertisement for a forgotten firm of marmalade manufacturers, E. & T. Pink of London; the oranges are winging their way from southern Spain.

PREMIER JAM POT COVERS

BRITISH MADE · BRITISH MADE

1 lb SIZE

STRAWBERRY JAM

1 D. PER PACKET

Recipes for making 28 kinds of JAMS AND MARMALADES

Recipes for making 28 kinds of JAMS AND MARMALADES

Contents – 24 GUMMED CIRCLES
24 WAXED CIRCLES – 24 LABELS

ASSORTED HOUSEHOLD
GUMMED LABELS

COCOA · TEA · JAM · PICKLE · PLUM · SALT · SUGAR

20 Sheets
165 Labels

All gummed and perforated

MADE IN ENGLAND

Left: Gummed labels from the 1930s for licking and sticking on jars, identifying the jam or jelly, and the date that it was made.

Above: Home-made jam was poured into a jar, a waxed circle was laid on top to prevent mould and then lidded with a gummed circle. Packet from the 1930s.

ENGLISH COUNTRY HOUSE JAMS, JELLIES, FRUITS, PICKLES & SAUCES
Direct from the FARM and FACTORY ARE A REAL LUXURY

PICKING STRAWBERRIES, FIFTEEN TONS PER DAY.

FAULDER & Co's LTD
TRADE SILVERPAN MARK
Henry Faulder & Co
SEVILLE ORANGE MARMALADE
STOCKPORT ENGLAND.
REGISTERED.

Above: For the increasingly urban population, fruit for making jams and jellies was often not readily available, hence the increase in goods made in the factory. Bill-head from c.1890.

Above: Faulder & Co., one of many marmalade manufacturers supplying Britain with its favourite breakfast preserve. Marmalade was more laborious than other kinds of preserve to make at home.

AFTERNOON TEA

The partaking of tea in the afternoon, accompanied by an assortment of thinly sliced bread-and-butter, sandwiches, biscuits and cakes, became an established tradition during Queen Victoria's reign; it served to stave off hunger mid-way between lunch and dinner, and was described in the 1893 edition of Mrs Beeton as one of the most useful and easy forms of entertainment.

'Little Teas', as they were called, consisted of a few plates of prettily arranged delicacies, usually served in the drawing room at a folding table set up in front of the fireplace. A small gathering of, predominantly, women assembled for polite exchange – and gossip – over a cup of tea. For a formal 'At Home' a table would be laid in the dining room, for as many as 200 guests. Foie gras sandwiches, mayonnaise of salmon, fancy biscuits and a cake iced with suitable or seasonal decoration might be on the menu, served with wine as well as tea.

In the 1930s a family tea would typically consist of potted salmon sandwiches, Bath buns or toasted teacakes, ginger snaps and cake. Although a variety of cakes could be bought or ordered from the shops, many housewives preferred to bake to their own recipes.

Top: 'To enjoy good health and save your health drink E. Temple's marvellous blended tea,' words printed on the back of this die-cut teacup and saucer of c.1900.

Above: The die-cut biscuit tin advertising Marsh & Co.'s Rich Cakes opens to reveal a calendar and postal rates for 1902.

Far left: 'Do you take Milk?'. An advertisement for the Express Dairy Company Ltd. featuring an Edwardian lady with her tea-set.

Left: Advertisement for the three varieties of Lyons 1d Choc Rolls, a popular teatime treat in the 1930s.

Above: Promotional postcard of c.1935 for Symington's Salanaise, to be made up into sandwich spread.

Above: Afternoon tea, a page from a give-away booklet from the biscuit-makers Peek, Frean & Co., c.1930. 'Ritz Assorted and Majestic Wafer please every taste.'

TEA

Tea, 'the cup that cheers', was part of the British way of life. As well as being taken for refreshment in polite society, it became the drink of the working people. Servants' wages varied according to whether tea was 'found', that is to say included, and they dried the leaves and reused them or sold them to buyers who came to the back door.

Loose tea leaves were stocked by grocers and blended for individual customers – hence Earl Grey tea – before packets of tea, already blended, began to appear in the shops, the first being Horniman's. The tea came only from China until Britain turned to its colonies, and from 1888 tea was imported into Britain in greater quantities from India, from Assam and Darjeeling in particular, and from Ceylon. By 1901 the average annual consumption of tea for each person was 6lb.

One heaped teaspoon per person and one for the pot was the recommended quantity for 'a nice cup of tea'. Whether milk should be added first or last was a matter much debated. J. Lyons & Co.'s teas were popular, competing with, among others, Ty-phoo tea, which claimed to be recommended by doctors 'in cases where ordinary tea has been strictly forbidden'; it did not cause flatulence and heartburn like 'coarse ordinary tea'.

Left: Die-cut chromolithograph scrap of a tea grocer with his scales and scoop for dispensing loose tea leaves, c.1880.

Below: Bill of 1871 from a Biggleswade merchant and tea dealer, stamped and receipted some six months later. The bill-head shows a Chinese tea merchant pointing to a tea clipper.

Right: Bill-head advertising Horniman's tea, c.1910. Frederick John Horniman, son of the founder of the tea business, set up the Horniman Museum in south London in 1901 with the proceeds from trading in tea.

Below: Advertisement for CWS tea at the time of George VI's coronation in 1937. 'Co-operatives, be upstanding and drink their Majesties' health in Co-operative Tea, the national beverage grown and distributed by your own organisation.'

Above: Bill-head advertising Ty-phoo tea, c.1935. Made from the edge of the leaf, the stalk containing tannin – which caused indigestion – was excluded. The tea was obtainable from chemists' shops.

CAKES

The Victorians had a cake recipe for every occasion, from the wedding breakfast to the schoolroom tea. Wedding Cake was an especially rich plum cake containing currants, raisins, candied peel, almonds and brandy; the most lavish had decoration built up in gum paste, its true glory being the topping of snow-white icing. A much plainer plum cake was described as 'suitable for sending to children at school'. Mrs Beeton's recipes for humbler households included Economical Cake and individual Scrap-cakes made with pig fat and ground allspice. Tipsy Cake was made with pieces of three- or four-day-old sponge cake laced with wine or sherry.

The cake named after Queen Victoria was a plain sponge flavoured with lemon rind; Francatelli introduced whipped cream, brandy, cinnamon and cherries into his recipe. Caraway seeds were the essential ingredient of the Seed Cake, much favoured in Victorian times. Dundee Cake was a fruit cake generously studded with almonds; it was among the most popular cakes produced by Huntley & Palmers at their Reading factory and sent all over the world. From the early 1930s some of their cakes could be bought in decorative tins.

At home, time and trouble was saved by the invention in the 19th century of baking powder, which replaced yeast and beaten egg as the raising agent, and later by sponge mixtures that came in a packet.

Left and below: Chromolithograph illustrations of cakes to be made at home including Victorian Twelfth Night Cake and Wedding Cake of the 1860s. Fancy ornaments could be bought ready made.

Above: Miniature recipe booklet produced by the baking powder manufacturer Wright, Crossley & Co. 'Not made in America' and 'Not made in Germany' suggests that it dates from the First World War.

Left: Advertisement for commercially made Dundee Cake and Cherry Cake with an illustration of the company's factory in London, c.1895.

Above: Full-page advertisement of c.1932 from the back of a woman's magazine proclaiming the convenience of labour-saving sponge mixture.

Right: Page from a booklet displaying the cakes manufactured by Huntley & Palmers in 1939, including the Sunray Cake with Art Deco icing.

ASSORTED BISCUITS

'Now that Huntley and Palmers, and Peek, Frean and Co. have brought the manufacture of biscuits to such perfection, there are but few people who consider it worthwhile making them at home; but for those few who prefer to have their own, as well as for those who have large families of children, we give a few well-tried recipes for simple kinds.' This was the situation as described in the 1893 edition of Mrs Beeton.

Deliciously tangy ginger biscuits, for which a recipe was given, continued to be home-made. They were a favourite of all ages and, in the shape of gingerbread men, were especially enjoyed by children. And they needed only five minutes in the oven. Ginger Nuts, as they were called, together with Osborne (named after Queen Victoria's Isle of Wight home), Abernethy, Nic-Nac and Gem biscuits, were among the cheaper kinds sold by Huntley & Palmers: 8d a pound in 1849. To begin with, biscuits made in the factory followed the recipes used in the home; later, a special department for experimentation was set up at the Huntley & Palmers factory in Reading to invent new varieties, in different shapes and with different flavours. The biscuits won prizes at the Paris Universal Exhibition in 1878 and again in 1900.

Top: Huntley & Palmers biscuit packet given in lieu of a farthing change, c.1885. The firm's beginnings date from the 1820s, when Joseph Huntley sold biscuits in Reading to stage-coach passengers.

Above: Packet label from Macfarlane, Lang & Co.'s Ottoman Biscuits, c.1900. The company turned from baking bread to making biscuits in 1886.

Below: Packets and tins of biscuits illustrated in a Huntley & Palmers catalogue of 1937. The tins, some designed as toys, added much to the appeal to purchasers.

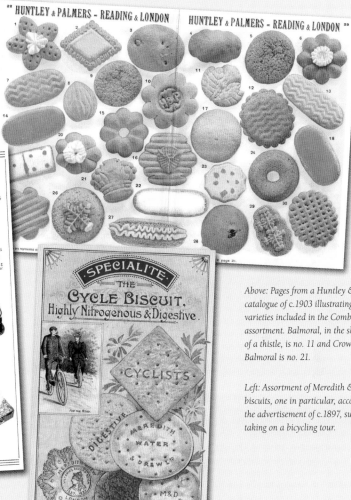

Above: Pages from a Huntley & Palmers catalogue of c.1903 illustrating the 30 varieties included in the Combination assortment. Balmoral, in the shape of a thistle, is no. 11 and Crown Balmoral is no. 21.

Left: Assortment of Meredith & Drew biscuits, one in particular, according to the advertisement of c.1897, suitable for taking on a bicycling tour.

CHILDREN'S FOOD

'I shall always consider that good food is to the body what education is to the mind,' wrote Soyer with reference to food suitable for children. He made an intensive study of children's dietary needs based on his own family. Like most Victorians, he was fearful of over-exciting his offspring with rich, flavourful food, and directed that the cook send bread and milk twice a day, every day, to the nursery. Lunch, or children's dinner, was to be bland, unexciting and monotonous: boiled mutton and turnips, for example, and occasionally salt beef and dumplings – and interminable milk puddings.

Mrs Craig, in the 20th century, concentrated on the value of a balanced diet for children 'if you want them to shine at school and at college, and if you want to send them well armed into the battle of life'. She preferred to give them raw, rather than cooked, vegetables.

A birthday tea consisted mainly of sweet things, though bread-and-butter was never omitted. There would be ice cream, jelly, sweet biscuits and of course a cake. Very thick icing apparently would do no harm so long as the main ingredients were wholesome. Cochineal-coloured buttons, candied fruit and dried cherries were favourite cake decorations.

Top: Invitation to a children's party dating from the turn of the century. To judge by the birthday cake pictured, with a ballerina on top, the party would have been for a girl.

Above: Packet labels for Peek, Frean's biscuits for children, c.1905.

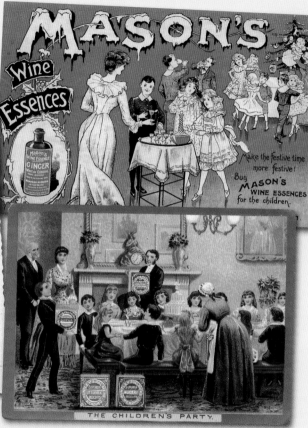

Below: Ginger, elderberry and orange were among the wine essences made by Mason's for children's parties. One bottle of the essence, costing 6d, made a gallon of the festive drink in the 1890s.

Above: Mealtime in the nursery, a leaflet encouraging the belief that thousands of children since 1880 had thrived on Express Dairy Milk.

Above: The Children's Party, an advertisement dating from c.1885 for Huntley & Palmers' biscuits, including tins of their Superior Little Folk and Superior Nursery assortments.

BISCUIT MAKERS

From the late 19th century, the variety of biscuits that could be bought, or ordered, from the grocer grew apace: by 1900 more than 400 varieties were being made by Huntley & Palmers alone.

Peek, Frean & Co., which had opened a factory in Bermondsey in 1866, introduced the Marie, Bourbon and Garibaldi biscuits; with their Chocolate Table biscuit of 1899 they introduced the novelty of a biscuit coated with chocolate.

One of the most popular biscuits was the Digestive, which was invented by Alexander Grant of Edinburgh in 1892 and sold by McVitie & Price as a health food. Grant convinced himself, and his purchasers, that the use of bicarbonate of soda as the raising agent made the biscuit good for the digestion. (In fact, once the bicarbonate of soda was baked all benefit was lost.) McVitie & Price's Chocolate Homewheat biscuit entered the market in 1925. In competition, William Crawford & Sons made a Digestive biscuit in the shape of an oval.

Biscuits represented one of the most successful of the Co-operative Wholesale Society's lines. During the 1930s it had 170 factories making their branded goods, and Co-op stores were within reach of almost everyone.

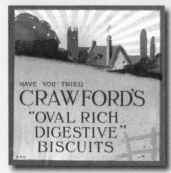

Above: Card issued in the 1920s by the Co-operative Wholesale Society advertising their Crumpsall Cream Crackers.

Left: A landscape featuring a wheatfield is the background to this c.1930 advertisement for the Digestive biscuits manufactured in Edinburgh by Crawford's.

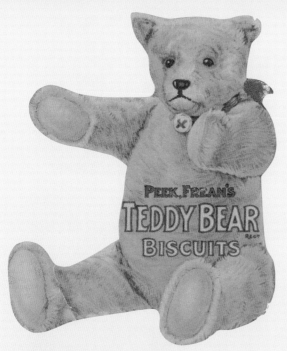

A Teddy Bear Puzzle

Place two Teddy Bear <u>Biscuits</u> side by side and say which is the larger. When you have decided, reverse the position of the <u>Biscuits</u> and it will be seen that the apparently larger becomes the apparently smaller. As a matter of fact they are both the same size.

Try this on your friends.

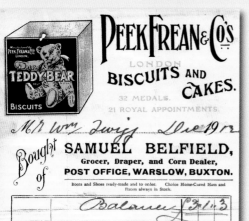

Above: Peek, Frean's die-cut advertisement of c.1905 for their Teddy Bear biscuits. On the back was printed instructions for a puzzle for children to try out on each other.

Left: Bill-head in use in 1912 by a grocer in Buxton who described himself as also a draper and corn dealer. Teddy Bear biscuits continued to be among the firm's most popular lines into the 1920s.

CHOCOLATE AND COCOA

Chocolate was unknown in Britain until the 17th century, but rapidly became popular as a luxurious hot drink when it was discovered how good it was mixed with sweetened milk. Cocoa powder and slabs of chocolate evolved as products after an invention by Conrad van Houten in 1828 of a screw press that removed the fatty cocoa butter from the dried and roasted cocoa bean kernel; cocoa powder was the result, and the extra cocoa butter was added to ground beans to make eating chocolate.

Victorian chocolate manufacture was dominated by Quaker families, principally Rowntree, Fry and Cadbury. As social reformers, they promoted chocolate as an alternative to the evils of alcohol. By 1866 the production of a pure and unadulterated cocoa – potato starch, arrowroot and sago flour were previously common additives – was under way, and it became one of the most widely advertised products of the age. It was sold as particularly beneficial to elderly people and children, with tags such as 'a healthy body is preparation for a healthy mind'. It was certainly more nourishing than the demon drink, and it was particularly recommended for breakfast.

Cocoa powder and chocolate were essential flavourings for cakes and puddings. Supplemented with vitamins and minerals, the basic formula was competitively adapted to make it even healthier in products such as Vi-Cocoa and Bourn-vita.

Top: Bee-shaped advertisement for Bournville Cocoa; on the back it states, 'Made in a Factory in a Garden', referring to the model factory village founded in the 1890s.

Above: Envelope in the shape of a tin that would have held a small sample of Bournville Cocoa, all part of the energetic promotion of the brand.

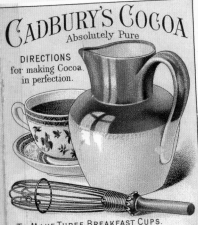

DIRECTION for making quickly.
FOR A BREAKFAST CUP.
Mix a teaspoonful dry with the same bulk of sugar, then pour on boiling water. It is improved by boiling. This Cocoa is perfectly pure.

CADBURY'S COCOA
IS SOLD ONLY IN TINS AND PACKETS

TINS AT
9d 1/-1/6
3/- 6/-

PACKETS
AT 3d
6d

"Absolutely Pure" therefore BEST." The Analyst.

CADBURY'S COCOA
Absolutely Pure

DIRECTIONS for making Cocoa in perfection.

TO MAKE THREE BREAKFAST CUPS.
In a quart jug (with rounded bottom and narrower neck for preference) mix 1½ dessert spoonfuls (½oz) of CADBURY'S COCOA with equal bulk of powdered white sugar and stir to a thin paste with a little boiling water.
Mix in an enamelled saucepan one breakfast cup of milk with two cups of water (cups to be about ¾ full) and boil with care. When on the boil pour this over the contents of the jug and whisk vigorously for a few seconds. Serve to table without delay.

Above: Leaflet of c.1890 on how to make cocoa; the reverse has a view of Cadbury's factory and an assurance that the cocoa contains 'no Kola, Malt, Hops, or Alkali'.

Right: Magazine advertisement from 1936 extolling the virtues of Bourn-Vita, a chocolate drink with added eggs, milk and barley malt 'for a refreshing sleep'.

Above: 1880s advertisement for Cadbury's Cocoa (before it was called Bournville). The child is reaching into the cupboard for her box of pure cocoa, which was sold in packets and tins 'By all respectable Grocers'.

PICNICS

Adding to the enchantment of eating out of doors and in the fresh air was the Victorian tradition of the gentlemen waiting on the ladies. The informal nature of the occasion did not mean that the kitchen was any the less busy beforehand, however. There was meat to be roasted, hams and tongue to be boiled and pressed, and pies to be made, all to be consumed cold on the day; there was lettuce to be picked over and washed, fruit to be selected for its ripeness; plain pastry biscuits to be baked, to go with the stewed fruit that travelled in corked glass bottles.

With the advent of the motor car, a drive into the countryside with a picnic in the boot was an attractive – even romantic – proposition. Picnic hampers were fitted with straps to hold eating implements and crockery secure; bottles and boxes of provisions had their own allocated place in the basket. There would be glasses for wine, beer, soda water and refreshing lemonade, and cups for tea. Not to be forgotten were salt, pepper, mustard, salad dressing and sugar – and a corkscrew. Bicycling and punting, cricket matches, and tennis, badminton and croquet parties provided other opportunities for putting together a selection of good things to eat and drink in the open air.

Top: 'With a Store of Good Wishes for You.' Chromolithograph die-cut Christmas greetings card of c.1880 in the form of a picnic hamper full of good things, including wicker-jacketed jars and bottles, and a cooked fowl, plum pudding and grapes.

Above: Picnic baskets for four and two persons from the Crowden & Garrod catalogue, 1903. The one on the right has fittings for tea, including a kettle and a teapot.

Below: Label of c.1840 for Effervescing Lemonade Powders. The powder wrapped in one of the blue papers was to be dissolved in half a pint of spring water, then the contents of one of the white papers added and the two stirred together.

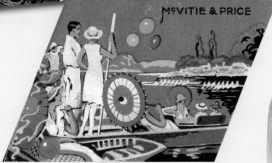

Above: Die-cut Thermos advertisement of c.1930. The vacuum flask was described as 'indispensable for all travellers, motorists, yachtsmen and all sportsmen. Keeps Hot drinks HOT for a day. Keeps Cold drinks COLD for many days.'

Above: McVitie & Price label of c.1930 indicates that the biscuits were exactly what was wanted on a boating expedition.

Left: Give-away of c.1910 for Chivers' Cambridge Lemonade, the 'Great Thirst Quencher'.

WATERS

For the Victorians, the dangers of drinking water from the local pump were well understood – particularly after 1854, when water was identified as the carrier of cholera. Piped water supplies were slow to reach rural areas and the poor areas of towns and cities; this influenced how much cooking and cleaning people did in their kitchens as well as the quality of their water. Just before the outbreak of the Second World War, at least ten per cent of the population was without a kitchen tap.

The solution to healthy drinking was to buy bottled water. A Swiss, Jacob Schweppe, invented a safe way of carbonating water at the end of the 18th century and established his company in England. Subsequently, a range of mineral waters – soda, seltzer, potass and lithia – vied with each other in their claims of healthiness and purity, and in popularity. Many of the bottling factories were based in traditional spa towns such as Malvern and Bath. Indian Tonic Water, containing malaria-defeating quinine, was introduced by Schweppes in 1870 and was an instant success. Testimonials abounded, the Pure Water Company of Battersea quoting *The Lancet*: 'We analysed a sample of this water, and obtained less than half a grain per gallon of solid matter, which as every chemist will understand, is practically nothing.'

Above: The Improved 'London Made' Syphon of c.1878, in quart or pint size, and Codd's Patent Globe-Stoppered Soda Water Bottle, 'easy and safe to open'.

Above: 1930s soda water labels from the necks of bottles.

Right: Business card for J. H. Cuff, c.1885. The Cuff family firm began in 1801 selling water by the glass from Holywell, Malvern, and expanded their business to Manchester.

Right: Label of c.1880 for Malvernia Sparkling Table Water, excellent 'for the gouty'. In an established spa town, small companies such as W. & J. Burrow could flourish.

Far right: Leaflet of c.1890 advertising the Pure Water Company of Battersea in London. It warned, 'Boiling water is not an adequate security against disease germs.'

Left: Promotional leaflet issued by the National Union of Mineral Water Manufacturers' Associations, c.1930. Doctors and scientists strongly advised that 'the internal matutinal [morning] bath is more necessary to the human system than regular external.'

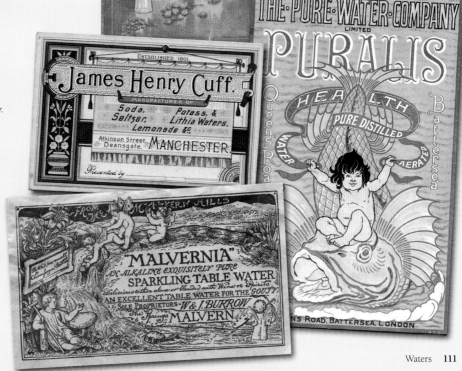

SOFT DRINKS

Many of the Victorian companies that sold mineral waters expanded their businesses into selling drinks such as lemonade and ginger beer. Sold in glass or stone bottles, they were popular for picnics, outings and summer events in the garden. Cookery books gave instructions for ginger beer brewed with yeast and lemonade made effervescent by the addition of carbonate of soda; increasingly these were also made commercially. So, too, were fruit cordials and syrups, the concocting of which had traditionally been the province of the housekeeper. Orgeat, a favourite 19th-century drink, involved pounding almonds with lemon essence and straining the mixture three times through a jelly bag. As kitchens became smaller, though, there was less space for such procedures, and it was simpler to buy the products ready-made.

A burgeoning temperance movement stimulated the market for non-alcoholic bottled drinks such as Champagne Ciderette and Orange Champagne manufactured by the Pure Water Company of Battersea, and lauded in the *Church Times* as having 'all the fizz and go of Moët without the disagreeable after consequences'. In the wake of American successes such as Dr Pepper and Coca-Cola (both dating from the 1880s), the British came up with the formulas for Vimto (1908, as Vim Tonic) and Tizer (1924), both sold as promoting health and fitness.

Top: 1930s bottle label in Art Deco style for Ginger Cordial, carefully labelled 'non-alcoholic' so as not to be confused with ginger wine.

Above: Bottle label for a non-alcoholic beer brought out in 1897, the Diamond Jubilee of Queen Victoria's accession to the throne.

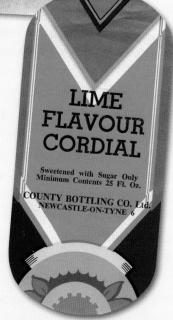

Above: Bottle label for Champagne Ciderette, an early 20th-century non-alcoholic drink, possibly thought suitable for ladies.

Left: Advertisement of c.1900 for a range of carbonated drinks such as Gingerette and Orange Champagne made by Brooke & Prudencio of Bristol.

Right: 1930s bottle label. Cordials made from fruits such as lime were in demand as an ingredient in modern cocktails.

INVALID COOKERY

'Kitchen physic' was the domain of the mother of the family: 'A truly loving and tender woman would rather prepare the food of her beloved and suffering child, or of her husband, than trust it to the care of an ordinary cook.'

It was vital not to put any strain on the digestive organs, and to this end broth, gruel, junket and jelly were appropriate for the invalid. To those who had to spend their time in bed, the arrival of the tray was one of the principal events of the day so should excite the interest of the patient: a stray flower or a prettily patterned plate would add to the appeal.

Beef tea was considered particularly efficacious: ½ lb lean diced meat and ½ pint of cold salted water were stewed in a slow oven for up to four hours and the liquid strained. Commercial products, such as Liebig's Extract of Beef and Brand's Essence of Chicken – originally devised by George IV's chef for the ailing king – were also available. Cornflour and Breadcrumb Puddings containing egg and milk could do no harm.

As stated in editons of Mrs Beeton: 'In case of infectious fever, all remains of food should at once be burnt, and on no account eaten by another person.'

Above: Cornflour, easier on the invalid's digestion than wheat flour, was supplied by Polson's to Queen Victoria, and the brand was recommended by Dr Lankester, Coroner for Middlesex. Advertisement of c.1869.

Left: Alexander Meat Juice Extractor (Dr Klein's Patent), from Crowden & Garrod's catalogue, 1903.

Below: Advertisement for Liebig Company's Lemco, with recipes on the back for invalid delicacies using Lemco Beef Tea and Lemco Invalid Jelly.

Above: Four invalid trays illustrated in a 1903 edition of Mrs Beeton. Pretty china, vases of flowers and fresh fruit might encourage the patient to contemplate the food set before him or her with a degree of enthusiasm.

Above: Nurse makes up a drink using Liebig's Peptone of Beef. Liebig products were promoted as a supplement for the malnourished, and here, in an advertisement of c.1890, as a 'nourishing and palatable drink for invalids and convalescents'.

NOURISHING FOOD

'When once the acute symptoms are over and the invalid is able to take more than mere sips of milk or water, the wasted body will require to be built up by a careful and strengthening diet,' wrote Florence Jack in her 1926 *Invalid Cookery Book*.

While food of a liquid nature was suitable in cases of severe illness, something more substantial was needed in convalescence. Tripe soup, containing potato, and vermicelli soup was recommended, and a fish soufflé or a fricassée of oysters was in order. Mac Fisheries put out a leaflet of recipes that included such temptations as Creamed Whiting and Fish in Custard.

Any proprietary food or drink that claimed to have a health benefit had a good chance of seeing healthy sales. Horlick's, which was invented in America for babies, was by the 1920s being advertised in England as a comforting remedy for sleeplessness and later as an energiser for growing schoolchildren. Ovaltine's claim was that it was the first convenient and complete milk fortifier to strengthen undernourished children, breastfeeding women, the weak and the infirm. Dr Wander, its Swiss inventor, cleverly included chocolate – an important industry in his country – as an ingredient, thereby making Ovaltine almost irresistible to children.

Above: 1920s advertisement for Harvo.
'Brown and sticky, nutty, sweet,
Wholesome, dainty, tea-time treat.
Luscious new, delightful stale,
Perfect food for people pale;
Filling brain and body cells
With the health which it compels.
Pre-digested Harvo cake,
Winter's scientific make.
Plain or full of fruit it's sold;
Worth its cost a hundredfold.'

Far right: Give-away from A. Wander, Manufacturing Chemists of London, recommending Ovaltine; the other side was to be used as a blotter.

Right: Alec's dismal performance at school was saved by Horlick's, and he was rewarded by his father with a brand-new bike. Advertisement of 1936.

Right: Paper bag with an advertisement for Ovaltine, c.1935. 'One cupful of this delicious beverage yields more nutriment than 3 eggs.'

Below and far right: Mac Fisheries in c.1920 produced a leaflet of invalid recipes for their customers. The humorous illustrations of the sick and suffering were contributed by the artist Dudley Jarrett.

BOVRIL, OXO AND MARMITE

The Victorians believed firmly in the strengthening and nourishing qualities of beef tea, but making it was a lengthy process. Bovril was an early commercialisation of the principle. A Scot called John Lawson Johnston created Johnston's Beef Fluid for the French army in 1870. Realizing the potential of his project, he established a company in Argentina to manufacture it and gave his product a more alluring name. Bovril was sold as either a delicious sandwich spread or as the basis of a hot drink; it was marketed as 'the most perfect form of nourishment at present known.'

Liebig's Extract of Meat was a similar product, and in 1899 the company launched Oxo as a cheaper version. An early advertising coup was to give Oxo Fluid Beef to athletes competing in the 1908 London Olympic Games. Foil-wrapped cubes appeared in 1910 and were an immediate success; they were distributed as part of the rations in the First World War.

Marmite looked just as beefy as these products but was actually made from vegetable matter, from a previously useless by-product of the brewing industry. Marmite was established as a company in 1902. Sales were boosted by the discovery of vitamins a decade later – Marmite was an excellent source of vitamin B – and thereafter its success was assured. Advertisements constantly reminded mothers of the benefit of Marmite to their children.

Above: Cover of a recipe booklet promoting Marmite and recommending its health-giving properties. Published in 1938, it included sections on invalid and vegetarian dishes.

I ALWAYS DRINK IT.

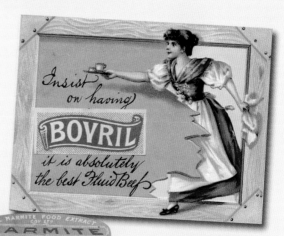

Insist on having **BOVRIL** it is absolutely the best Fluid Beef

Right and below: Comical novelty advertisement for Bovril, c.1910. The reverse of the top-hatted man turns into a victory column suggesting the energy-giving qualities of the product.

BOVRIL

THE CHALLENGE CUP OPEN TO ALL THE WORLD

BOVRIL IS STRENGTH

BOVRIL IS POWERFUL AND INVIGORATING

MARMITE

(A PURE VEGETABLE EXTRACT.)

Awarded 2 Gold Medals.

The Best and Cheapest Extract for the Kitchen, for Soups, Sauces, Gravies, &c.

" THE LANCET " says:
"This entirely vegetable extract possesses the same nutrient value as a well-prepared Meat Extract."

" THE HOSPITAL " says:
"We regard Marmite as likely to prove of great value in the treatment of the sick."

OBTAINABLE AT ALL GROCERS AND STORES.

THE MARMITE FOOD EXTRACT CO. LTD

MARMITE

LONDON & BURTON-ON-TRENT

MARMITE

TRADE MARK

MARMITE

MARMITE FOOD EXTRACT Co Limited
WORKS - BURTON-ON-TRENT.

OFFICES: 40. MINCING LANE. LONDON. E.C.

Above: Advertisement of c.1895 suggesting that a cup of hot Bovril is good for emergency siuations such as falling through ice.

Above: Advertisement of c.1910 in the shape of the original earthenware Marmite pot; it was then also available in tubes. Glass jars were introduced in the 1920s.

Right: Competitors Oxo and Bovril both produced advertising scraps in the 1900s in the shape of beefy-looking ox and bull heads.

FIRST PRIZE & CHAMPIONSHIP OXO

DINNER PARTIES

The pages in editions of Mrs Beeton on the subject of dinner were likely to be well thumbed by socially ambitious housewives wanting to copy what went on in the best circles. In 1861 Mrs Beeton gave them a clue when she described the increasingly fashionable style of dining *à la russe*. Here, diners were waited on individually by a servant, and each dish with its accompaniments represented a complete course. With the older style of dining *à la française*, a course consisted of several dishes placed on the table at the same time for diners to help themselves and their neighbours. It was, literally, a spread. Suggested menus were given for both in the original *Book of Household Management*.

When choosing the menu, the mistress needed to make sure that some dishes could be prepared in advance. What was nerve-wracking, in fact impossible, for the cook was when several dishes had to be cooked at the same time, each one up until the last moment. 'For instance,' it was pointed out in *Cassell's Dictionary*, 'fried oysters, kromeskies, mutton-cutlets, and a savoury omelet, would be a sore trial to a cook were they ordered as four entrées together.' (Kromeskies were croquettes made of meat or fish minced, rolled in bacon or calf's udder and then fried.)

Top: Dishes for a dinner party from an 1869 edition of Mrs Beeton, Filet of Beef à la Jardinière in the middle and Calf's Head Garnished at the bottom.

Above: Dish and water jug illustrated in the catalogue of the 1862 International Exhibition in London.

MENU

Oysters.

White Soup.   Clear Soup.

Salmon.   Whitebait.

Fricassée of Lobster.   Sweetbreads.

Roast Lamb.   Spring Chickens.

Wild Duck.

Trifle.   Meringues.   Jelly.

ICES.

14 Park Circus,
28th January, 1892.

Above: Table laid with eight place settings complete with glasses and napkins for a modified form of dinner à la russe, a colour plate of c.1880.

Above right: Menu for dinner at 14 Park Circus for 28th January 1892. With formal dining, a menu would be placed on the table before each diner. Here, oysters were served as a first course, and dinner concluded with trifle, meringues and jelly, followed by ices.

Right: Dinner table, a fold-out illustration from a 1903 edition of Mrs Beeton. 'At the present time there is quite a furore for original designs for the ornamentation of our tables with flowers and foliage.'

SERVANTLESS DINNER

During the years when housewives were learning to cope with very little or no help, dinner was reduced in scale and elaboration, and the menu no longer pretentiously French as was sometimes the case in Edwardian times. For the more sophisticated, it was to be the era of artful simplicity.

Numerous courses, heavy roasts and sickly sauces were out. Cold hors d'oeuvres, already on the table when the diners arrived, were more than ever the fashionable start to a formal dinner: iced melon with a sprinkling of ginger, oysters, caviar or smoked salmon. Avocado pears were discovered, salads were concocted from previously unthought-of combinations of vegetables and fruit. Savouries such as anchovy straws, believed to appeal to the men, might follow the sweet or even replace it. According to *Warne's Model Cookery and Housekeeping Book* in 1929, 'The mistress of the house [who might also have been the cook] usually serves the soup, vegetables and sweet, while the master serves the fish, and meat, poultry or game, unless they are handed round by the parlourmaid.'

Flowers rather than fruit-laden centrepieces were the principal ornaments of the dinner table. Complicated styles of napkin-folding were illustrated in books on household management, and linen manufacturers' leaflets promoted instant expertise.

Above: Joints illustrated in a 1903 Mrs Beeton: from the top, Sirloin of Beef, Boiled Beef, Roast Aitchbone of Beef and Roast Ribs of Beef.

The Fan Closed

Fold the serviette in four (longways); as in Fig. 15, then fold it across the breadth, commencing at one end and folding from and to yourself in folds nearly two inches broad when folded, as in Fig. 16 hold the serviette firmly in the left hand with the end with the two double edges up; then with the right hand pull down the inside folds to make right-angles with the top;

FIG. 15.

FIG. 16. turn the napkin in the hand, and do the same with the inside folds on the other side. This should make two rows of points, one point coming between two others. The serviette must then be put in a hockglass or tumbler. The fan must be folded with the greatest neatness and exactitude, or it will look very bad.

ROBINSON & CLEAVER, BELFAST. COPYRIGHT.

The Lily

FIG. 5. FIG. 6.

Fold the serviette in two cornerways, as Fig. 5; then turn up the two corners of the dotted lines; then fold up the corner of the square at the line J, and then turn the points over, as in Fig. 6. Tuck one of the lower corners into the other, as in combined figure.

ROBINSON & CLEAVER, BELFAST. COPYRIGHT.

Above: Pages from a booklet of detailed instructions on how to fold table napkins, or serviettes, for decorative effect, put out by Robinson & Cleaver, linen manufacturers and merchants of Belfast in c.1900. The Lily and the Fan were two of the designs illustrated.

Below: The Evening Meal, an illustration in a give-away booklet on indoor games from Peek, Frean, c.1930.

Above: Strawberry Cream, as recommended for a summer dinner in Warne's Everyday Cookery, 1929. It needed ½ pint of fruit purée, ½ pint of double cream and 1oz of gelatine.

Above: Hors d'oeuvres, also illustrated in Warne's Everyday Cookery, 'should be small and daintily served'.

SOUP

Rarely did a Victorian or Edwardian menu for dinner not begin with a soup course: virtue was made of necessity, and it did not escape the notice of the housekeeper that soup was an excellent way of 'utilising material that would otherwise be wasted'. Soups were classified as broths, clear soups, thick soups, pottages and purées. Broths were the most basic: meat off-cuts such as bones and skin, brisket, ox-cheek and turkey trimmings were boiled, often with the addition of pearl barley or rice. Fine clear soups, or consommés, were the most gastronomically tricky. They were made with strong, pure beef stock with a jellifying ingredient such as cow's heel that had been carefully strained and then clarified to transparency by adding beaten egg white. There was resistance to vegetable soups as 'unpleasing to the English palate'.

Boiling a stock pot was simple on old-fashioned ranges, and the timing given in most recipes was usually at least four hours; Turtle Soup, one of the most favoured, was reckoned in *Warne's Model Cookery and Housekeeping Book* (1869) to take over six hours. Short cuts in the form of meat extracts and desiccated soups were particularly welcome with the advent of gas and electricity, which for lengthy cooking times cost more than coal or coke.

Above: Chromolithograph advertising scrap, c.1900, for Edwards' Desiccated Soups, the packets cost 1d each, and the flavours were Brown, White, Tomato and Gravina.

Left: Symington's manufactured packet soups from the early 20th century. The recipe leaflet of c.1925 suggested ways of using them as sauces.

Left: Colour plate from Mrs Beeton, 1903, showing bowls of soup ranging from Mutton Broth to Consommé à la Julienne.

Below: Armour was a company based in Chicago, which was the epicentre of the American meat industry. Chromolithograph advertisement, c.1905.

Right: Kent's Patent Soup Strainer, from Warne's Model Cookery and Housekeeping Book of 1869. 'Useful for procuring the transparency so much required by fashion in modern soups.'

SOUP MAKING – A PLEASURE,
WITH ARMOUR'S EXTRACT.

ARMOUR & CO.
EXTRACT OF BEEF
CHICAGO,
U.S.A.

ARMOUR'S
EXTRACT OF BEEF
ARMOUR & CO.
Chicago, U.S.A.

FISH

Fish was acknowledged to be 'less satisfying and stimulating than butcher's meat', but fishmongers flourished. Many families observed the custom of eating fish and no meat on Fridays, and few properly arranged dinners before the First World War omitted to have a fish course – a whiting soufflé, brill with lobster sauce or oyster patties. Cheap fish for the poor included eel, herring, hake and dab, while highly valued fish such as sturgeon and lobster were the centrepieces of grand buffets and ball suppers. Cod was much admired, specifically the sounds and cheeks: 'epicures look for the sounds, the glutinous parts about the head and tongue'. Freshwater fish, particularly grayling, tench and carp, were for families living in the country far from the sea, their muddy taste obliterated by a long soak in salted water.

Vast catches of herring from the North Sea gave fishing towns such as Yarmouth and Grimsby a busy trade in smoked fish. They sent kippers, or 'red herrings', bloaters and buckling all over the country. For some people, sardines, an early success of the canned-food industry, and fish paste were the nearest they got to fresh fish.

Above: Lowestoft identified strongly with its kipper industry. The die-cut holiday souvenir of c.1905 opens to reveal a cascade of holiday views including the fish market.

Left: Victorian fish dishes from an 1893 edition of Mrs Beeton illustrating the much-prized Cod's Head.

Below left: Promotional postcard, c.1910, for Skippers Sardines, a firm founded by Angus Watson, who spotted canning potential in the small fish thrown away by Norwegian fishermen.

Below: Watson used the Sailor brand name for tinned salmon, and also for fish paste, which was increasingly popular for sandwiches. Promotional postcard, c.1925.

Above: Victorian fish dishes from Warne's Model Cookery and Housekeeping Book, 1869, including a centrepiece of Lobster. The silver dishes hold Scalloped Oysters and Crimped Skate

MEAT

One of the most important responsibilities of the Victorian housekeeper was finding a good butcher, since meat was usually included in the menu for breakfast, lunch and dinner. Despite a system of government inspection, it was not uncommon for unscrupulous tradesmen to sell meat from diseased animals.

Beef was considered 'the national meat', but mutton was thought to be more digestible; its flavour was considered more delicate and it was better adapted to the needs of persons who follow sedentary occupations. Pork (with rabbit and hare) was what one writer called 'cottage meat'; country families often kept a pig fattened on kitchen scraps, and bacon was a staple.

A cheap alternative was tinned corned beef from Fray Bentos, Uruguay, imported in quantity from 1862; but the price of meat really fell in the 1880s with the advent of refrigerated shipping. Lamb from Australia and New Zealand, pork from America and beef from Argentina became available all year round.

Fresh or frozen, little was wasted: ox-cheek mould, stewed ox palates, fried veal tendons, mutton brain and tongue pudding and pigs' ears in jelly all feature in a 1903 edition of Mrs Beeton, beside the usual large joints. Shortages during the First World War broke the national habit of large-scale meat consumption.

Above: Advertisement from the 1890s for very popular Paysandu Ox Tongues, named after the town in Uruguay where they were canned. 'Every tongue guaranteed by McCall & Co. Ltd.'

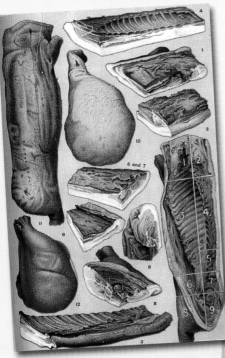

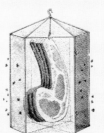

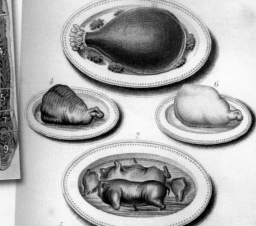

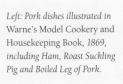

Above: Items from the Crowden & Garrod catalogue of 1903, the Sexagon and Fly Cheat folding meat cages and the Superior meat safe.

Above: Detailed information on different cuts of meat was given in all housekeeping and cookery manuals; illustrated in this 1903 edition of Mrs Beeton are joints of ham and bacon.

Left: Pork dishes illustrated in Warne's Model Cookery and Housekeeping Book, 1869, including Ham, Roast Suckling Pig and Boiled Leg of Pork.

ICE CREAMS

To serve elaborate and decorative iced creams and iced puddings at a Victorian dinner or ball supper was the height of elegance. Until the 1840s the only available ice came from ice-houses filled during winter frosts but, once a steady supply of ice from North America was established, these confections were easier to create.

Left: Detail from a bill-head from 1867 illustrating Torrey's Arctic Freezer, one of the many patent freezing devices on the market.

The technique was to put the ingredients into 'freezing machines', which were packed with ice and salt or 'freezing powder'. Contraptions such as Ash's Piston Freezing Machine were described in 1869 as 'pretty little machines [that] can be used by the lady herself, with the greatest ease ... a pleasant and amusing task ... and at a very small expense iced creams, puddings etc. can be produced whenever required.' Perennially popular were Nesselrode Frozen Pudding (custard with diced fruit) and ice creams made with brown bread, ratafia biscuits, cinnamon, tea and fruit, as well as sorbets made with champagne and maraschino cherries, iced mousses and bombes.

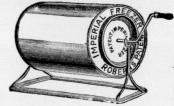

Left: Imperial ice-cream freezer, from a spring hardware catalogue put out by Crowden & Garrod, 1903.

Mrs Marshall's *Book of Ices* includes recipes for such curiosities as ices perfumed with jasmine and bergamot, and a frozen curried fish soufflé that she named Soufflé of Curry à la Ripon. Later, manufacturers such as Walls supplied ice cream directly to people's doors.

Right: Marshall's Patent Ice Cave was recommended for taking ice creams on picnics.

Above: W for Walls, a card to be put in the window requesting a call from the ice cream salesman. 'Stop Me and Buy One' was the salesmen's slogan when the rounds started in 1923.

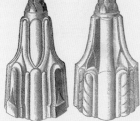

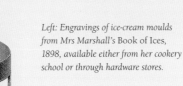

Left: Engravings of ice-cream moulds from Mrs Marshall's Book of Ices, 1898, available either from her cookery school or through hardware stores.

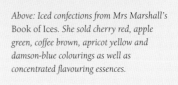

Above: Iced confections from Mrs Marshall's Book of Ices. She sold cherry red, apple green, coffee brown, apricot yellow and damson-blue colourings as well as concentrated flavouring essences.

Ice Creams **131**

JELLIES

Trembling, glistening jellies in fanciful shapes were the ornaments of many a dinner and supper table. Mouth-watering confections of different transparent hues were described by Eliza Acton: a pale pink jelly made with fresh young rhubarb was a favourite; while one of her specialities was a dish of quartered oranges filled with alternate stripes of jelly – one natural and one coloured with cochineal, each being allowed to set in the mould before the next was added. Fresh berries, peaches and apricots were the colourful ingredients of Mrs Beeton's Macédoine de Fruits.

The setting agent for desserts and savouries used in the early years of Queen Victoria's reign was the separated jelly from calves' feet broth, the making of which caused one of the most unpleasant kitchen smells. Conical flannel bags were used to strain the liquid, which had then to be clarified with the shells and whisked white of egg.

The commercial production of ready-to-use gelatine speeded up the process. Sales of bottled jelly were overtaken in the 20th century by jelly flakes and cubes of condensed jelly that required only to be dissolved in boiling water.

Top: Sweet Macédoine de Fruits and savoury Jelly à la Bellevue, illustrations from an 1893 edition of Mrs Beeton.

Above: Rowntree's packet of table jellies. A patent for the new jelly in cubes was applied for in 1930.

Left: 1933 advertisement for Chivers' Jellies, 'economical, nourishing and easily transformed into an endless variety of tempting warm-weather dishes.'

Below: Chromolithograph die-cut advertisement dating from the turn of the century for Rizine Co.'s Fruit Jelly Flakes in six flavours: lemon, raspberry, orange, strawberry, cherry and 'pine-apple'.

Above: Advertisement of c.1885 for gelatine from the well-established firm of J. & G. Cox Ltd. Commercial production of gelatine did away with the necessity of making it at home in a lengthy and disagreeably smelly process.

BLANCMANGES

'Blanc-manger', as described by Francatelli, was flavoured with Jordan almonds and bitter almonds. These were boiled together, released from their skins and pounded to a creamy pulp with sugar and orange-flower water. Diluted with water and strained, this was the ingredient that, mixed with isinglass, made for an excellent dessert.

Mrs Beeton's recipe included milk, cream and lemon rind as well as almonds. 'Noyeau, Maraschino, Curaçoa, or any favourite liqueur, added in small proportions, very much enhances the flavour of this always favourite dish.' Thus 'improved', the blancmange was evidently destined for the grown-ups rather than for children. Mrs Beeton's cheap version, originally costing 8d instead of 3s 3d, was flavoured with bay leaves instead of almonds. Coloured blancmanges made with powder from a packet came on the market later.

Moulds for the jellies and blancmanges came in many different shapes and sizes; some had crenellations so tall and complicated that it is hard to believe that the creations did not collapse as soon as they were turned out. To ensure a smooth and glossy surface, the moulds were best soaked in cold water or oiled before use.

Left: Cerebos were the makers of 'blanc-mange' powder and a number of other easy-to-use products. This packet label of c.1925 shows a twin-flavoured and coloured dessert made in a turreted mould.

Below: Packet label of c.1925 for four kinds of Carltona blancmange powder. The opaque blancmanges were popular with children, who might be allowed to help make them.

Below: Full-page advertisement for blancmange and jelly moulds of variously complicated shape that appeared in an 1877 edition of Francatelli's The Cook's Guide and Housekeeper's & Butler's Assistant.

Above: Alfred Bird & Sons Ltd, of Birmingham, were manufacturers of a number of easy-to-use cooking products that became extremely popular in Victorian times; one of them was blancmange powder. Bird's custard powder was the best known.

USE **Birds Specialities.**

BIRD'S CUSTARD POWDER *for your Custards.*

BIRD'S BLANC-MANGE POWDER *for your Blanc-manges.*

BIRD'S CRYSTAL JELLY POWDER *for your Jellies.*

BIRD'S EGG POWDER *for your Cakes, Buns, &c.*

BIRD'S BAKING POWDER *for your Bread, Pastry, Puddings &c.*

COPYRIGHT   ENTERED AT STATIONERS' HALL.

TIN MOULDS.

No. 73.   No. 74.   No. 75.

5½ in., 4s.
No. 77.

5½ in., 5s. 6d.

No. 76.
... 9d.

5¼ in., 3s. 9d.

No. 80.

5½ in., 4s.

No. 78.

6 in., 4s. 9d.

No. 79.

5¼ in., 4s. 9d.
No. 82.

5½ in., 4s.

No. 81.

5¼ in., 4s.
No. 84.

5½ in., 4s. 4d.

No. 83.

5½ in., 3s. 9d.

5½ in., 5s.

SPECIMEN PAGE FROM 'BOOK OF MOULDS.'

Blancmanges   **135**

BEERS, WINES AND SPIRITS

The huge amount of food eaten in the 19th century was accompanied by equally copious quantities of drink. Some brewing and distilling was done in the kitchen quarters, and recipe books included drinks such as Apple Wine, Cowslip Wine, Cherry Brandy, Birch Beer (made with birch bark, hops, pimento, golden syrup and yeast) and liqueurs – hawthorn blossom steeped in brandy, for instance, and Raspberry Gin. These, together with the standard contents of the cellar – brandy, whisky, rum, sherry and port as well as wine (invariably French or German) – went into cups and punches. Bishop (hot sherry flavoured with lemon) and Negus (hot port, lemon and nutmeg) were popular in winter, and for summer iced Moselle Cup (with curaçao and seltzer water). Champagne was safe: 'its intoxicating effects are rapid, but exceedingly transient'.

Alcohol also appears in recipes for 'efficacious tonics' – one in the *Epicure's Alamanac* of 1842 includes gentian root, juniper berries, coriander and cardomom seeds infused in five quarts of brandy and strained through blotting paper after a fortnight. An 1882 book on party-giving suggests 'wine and water' – three bottles of sherry to six quarts of lemonade – for juvenile parties; it was to be served with cake. By 1936 *The Ideal Home* was deploring the disappearance of cellars and regretting that wine must be stored in the larder.

Left: Advertisment for the Perfection Bottle Clip, a stopper device to retain the bubbles in opened bottles of champagne or ale, c.1885.

Left: Price card from a French champagne exporter, c.1890. Contemporary advice on giving dinner parties was to allow a half bottle for a man, one-third for a lady.

BEERS
WINES
SPIRITS
WATERS

DIRECT FROM
LOVIBONDS
TO
YOUR DOOR

JOHN LOVIBOND & SONS LTD
Greenwich & Salisbury
and 50 Branches.

Below: Selection of corkscrews from Crowden & Garrod's 1903 catalogue of hardware; the brush attachments were to dust the bottles retrieved from the cellar.

CORKSCREWS. (cc)

No. 563.
Polished Boxwood.
Stout Nickel-plated
Cut Worm.
On Cards of ½ doz.
9/ per doz.

THE "HERCULES,"
Nickel-plated,
No. 15, 6/ per doz.

THE "IMPROVED
HERCULES."
Superior,
Nickel-plated.
No. 15A, 9/6 per doz.

THE
No. 16,

W. & G. PETERS,
IMPORTERS
OF
FOREIGN WINES & SPIRITS.

W. & G. PETERS

BIRMINGHAM.

THORNE LTD
NINE ELMS
1906

Nine Elms Brewery Stores,
89, Vicarage Road,
NEASDEN, N.W.

Above: Leaflet from Lovibonds, originally Victorian brewers but, by the 1920s, a successful chain of wine merchants with delivery vans.

Right: Advertisement for Thorne's Ales and Stouts, sold in crates of four in 1906.

Above: Engraved trade card for a wine merchant in Birmingham, c.1840. Such cards commonly illustrated their impressive premises.

CHRISTMAS

The busiest time in the kitchen was in the weeks leading up to Christmas. Biscuits and a Christmas cake were baked, or bought from a shop selling a range with special Christmas decorations. Mince pies and mulled wine were made, ready to be given to carol singers who came to the door, and cheer them on their way from house to house. The warming brew was prepared by boiling cloves, grated nutmeg, cinnamon or mace in the equivalent of a large cupful of water to extract their flavour, and adding sugar and a pint of red wine, then bringing it all to boiling point. The drink was given out in conical tin 'mulls' used only for this purpose.

'Christmas is coming, the goose is getting fat' are the opening words of a favourite carol. Roast goose – with stuffing of apples, onions, sage and lemon-thyme to make it go further for a large gathering – was traditional Christmas fare in the south of England, and goose clubs helped people to save up during the rest of the year. In the north people were likely to feast on roast beef. Turkeys, which had arrived from America many years before, became popular towards the end of the 19th century.

Above: Christmas greetings card of c.1875 showing a couple choosing their Christmas dinner from a market stall.

Above: Leaflet of c.1910 for Chivers' mincemeat, which, it was claimed, 'excels home made'.

Right and below right: Label from a Lyons' fruit cake in a special Christmas wrapping, c.1930, and a label for Huntley & Palmers' Christmas assortment of biscuits from 1883.

Christmas   **139**

CHRISTMAS PUDDING

An annual ceremony was involved in the making of the Christmas Pudding. The children gathered in the kitchen to stir the moist and delicious mixture of dried fruit, breadcrumbs, suet, eggs, sugar and brandy, and to make a wish. Christmas charms would be added to the ingredients: silver three-penny pieces; a ring to foretell a marriage; a horseshoe for luck; and a variety of sliver-thin silver animals.

'The plum pudding is a national dish, and is despised by foreign nations because they can never make it fit to eat,' it was declared in *Cassell's Dictionary of Cookery*. 'In almost every family there is a recipe for it, which has been handed down from mother to daughter through two or three generations, and which never has been equalled, much less surpassed by any other.' The entry continues, 'It is usual, before sending it to table, to make a little hole in the top and fill it with brandy, then light it, and serve it in a blaze. In olden time a sprig of arbutus, with a red berry on it, was stuck in the middle, and a twig of variegated holly, with berries, placed on each side. This was done to keep away witches.'

Above: Christmas Pudding on a stand, an illustration from The Modern Householder, *published by Warne in 1872.*

Left: Label for a tin of traditional Christmas Pudding, encircled by flames and topped with a twig of holly, posted from New Zealand in c.1890. On it are the words 'belly have jolly good duff enough whether it be hot or cold.'

Below: Cover of a recipe leaflet of c.1920 produced by Latham & Co., Ltd, Liverpool, manufacturers of Cakeoma. The recipes given inside for Christmas cake, puddings and mincemeat include the use of a packet of Cakeoma in each one.

RECIPES

for

CHRISTMAS

CAKES & PUDDINGS

Above: Raphael Tuck & Sons Christmas greetings card of c.1905 showing a mother and her children, with the cook and kitchen maid, gathered in the kitchen for the ceremony of stirring the Christmas Pudding.

INDEX

ACKNOWLEDGEMENTS AND SOURCES

The ephemera reproduced in this book are from the collection of Amoret Tanner, to whom Elizabeth Drury and Philippa Lewis are immensely grateful. Quoted material and other illustrations are from the following:

Acton, Eliza, *Modern Cookery for Private Families* (London, 1856 edn)

Allen, M. L., *Breakfast Dishes for Every Morning of Three Months* (London, 1886)

Beeton, Mrs Isabella, *Mrs Beeton's Book of Household Management* (Oxford, abridged edn 2000)

Beeton, Mrs Isabella, *The Book of Household Management* (London, 1869 edn)

Beeton, Mrs Isabella, *Beeton's Every-day Cookery and Housekeeping Book* (London, 1893 and 1903 edns)

Cassell's Dictionary of Cookery (London, n.d.)

Cobbett, Anne, *The English Housekeeper* (London, 1842)

Craig, Elizabeth, *Cookery Illustrated and Household Management* (London, 1936)

Craig, Elizabeth, *The Way to a Good Table: Electric Cookery* (London, 1937)

Dolby, Richard, *The Cook's Dictionary and Housekeeper's Directory* (London, 1833)

Forster Murphy, Shirley, *Our Homes and How to Make them Healthy* (London, Paris and New York, 1883)

Francatelli, Charles, *A Plain Cookery Book for the Working Classes* (London, 1852)

Francatelli, Charles, *The Cook's Guide and Housekeeper's & Butler's Assistant* (London, 1877 edn)

Frazer, Mrs J. G., *First Aid to the Servantless* (Cambridge, 1913)

Haweis, Mrs, *The Art of Housekeeping* (London, 1889)

Herbert, A. Kenney, *Fifty Breakfasts* (London, 1892)

Herbert, A. Kenney, *Fifty Dinners* (London, 1895)

Hooper, Mary, *Nelson's Home Comforts* (London, 1885 edn)

Jack, Florence B., *Cookery for Every Household* (Edinburgh, 1914)

Jekyll, Lady, *Kitchen Essays with Recipes and their Occasions* (London, 1922)

Jewry, Mary (editor), *Warne's Model Cookery and Housekeeping Book* (London, 1869)

Marshall, Mrs A. B., *Mrs Marshall's Cookery Book* (London, 1897 edn)

Marshall, Mrs A. B., *Book of Ices* (London, 1898 edn)

Murray, Ross (editor), *The Modern Householder: A Manual of Domestic Economy in all its Branches* (London, 1872)

Panton, J. E., *From Kitchen to Garrett* (London, 1888)

Poole's Family Account Book for 1837

Punch magazine

Soyer, Alexis, *A Shilling Cookery for the People* (London, 1855)

Soyer, Alexis, *The Modern Housewife* (London, 1851 edn)

Soyer, Alexis, *Soyer's Charitable Cookery* (London, 1848)

Timbs, J. J., *Hints for the Table: or, The Economy of Good Living* (London, 1869)

Victorian Shopping, facsimile edn. of *Harrods Catalogue*, 1895, intro by Alison Adburgham (Newton Abbot, 1972)

Wijey, Mrs Mabel (editor), *Warne's Everyday Cookery* (London, 1929)

White, Florence, *Good Things in England* (London, 1932)